Tools of Light,
Gifts from the ALB's

Author
Lady Wolfen Mists

Library of Congress Control Number
ISBN: 978-0-9790662-3-8
Copyright Date: April 26 2015

Copyright © Lady Wolfen Mists
Cover © fbc24 - Fotolia.com
Page 99 Public Domain

All rights reserved. No part of this book may be reproduced by any means (including electronic) or in any form whatsoever without written permission from the publisher and author, except for **very brief** quotations embodied in literary articles or reviews

Silver Hoofs Inc
Fargo, North Dakota

http://www.silverhoofs.com

Printed in the United States Of America

Dedication

This Book is dedicated to All those Light Workers out there who wish to change the world and make things better. These tools are yours for the making, so use them wisely and fight the darkness that takes our hope and our life. That darkness that gives us hopelessness, depression and desperation. If you want to work with the Angels of Love and Light and make a difference this book is for you.

Contents
Tools of Light, Gifts from the ALBs

Why I call Them ALB's	12
Grid of healing water post	13
Grid of Healing water Instructions	16
Keepers of Abundance Shrine	21
Post on Open a Healing tool	30
Open a healing channel tool instructions	32
Spirit Shield Wreath Post	40
Spirit Shield instructions	41
Chest Guard Tool	48
Energy Influx Recipe	57
How to make negative entities run	59
Celestite Tool ribbon of Light	63
3 feather Prayer Protector	67
Align the Light Waters	72
Unbreakable Will Oil	74
Blue Kyanite Scalpel	77
Light Empowered Bracelet	80
Healing Glass: Power of 3	84
Let Blessings Flow tube	87
Chain breaker	90
Random Acts Of Kindness Cards	93

Seals, Symbols

Michael seal	101
Raphael seal	102
Gabriel seal	103
Uriel seal	104

Ariel seal	105
Isda Nurture Seal	106
Risnuch seal	107
Symbol for Angelic Legion	109
Animal Protection symbol	112
Loved One Protection symbol	113
Reverse Negativity symbol	114
Manifest and Protect symbol	115
Remove Negativity & Maintain a clean positive House recipe	116
Trap Negativity Symbol	117
Positive Abundance, Wealth, Knowledge & More	118
All I touch becomes Gold	119

Oils, Sprays & Dusts

Unbreakable Will Oil	124
Essence of Light Oil	125
Moon Willow Oil	126
All Angel Anointing Oil	127
Broken Wings Oil	128
Michael's Lit 'em up Spray	130
Empath's Auto Shield Spray Impenetrable	131
Self Defense Dust	132

Waters

Metaphysical Correct Holy Water	138
Blessing Water	139
Raphael Spirit Scrubber Water	140
Raphael Life's Green Fire Water	141

Tea Lights

About Tea Lights	144
Bound to the Light Tea Light	146
The Angelic Essence Tea Light	147
Sending out my Will to the Angels Tea Light	148

Affirmations and Chants/Prayers

Angelic Affirmation Fortune Cookies	152
Affirmation to lift us up	154
Chants/Prayers	158

Fabric Tools

How these tools are used	164
To Banish Negativity/Demons	165
Blessing of a New Life or Home	167
Protection from all forms of Extreme Weather	168

Bring Wealth & Gifts to someone	169
Material, Spiritual, Mentally	
Surrounded By the Light	170
Legion Of Light Pillow	172

Tools that don't fit anywhere else

DARKNESS vs dark/shadow self; What they are	178
Anti-Vampire Sachets	180
Sacred Ground Resins	181
Angel World Terrarium	182

Acts of Light for the Year

January-*Tasty Love abounds*	186
February- *"I Appreciate you" eye pads*	187
March- *Life renewal*	188
April- *Angelic Stress reducer*	188
May- *Flowers Bloom*	189
June- *Ringing Protection Bells*	190
July - *Shining Star Reminder*	191
August- *Feed the Body the soul will follow*	193
September - *Companion time*	194
October- *Make a "See U "Bug Hug*	194
November- *You Rock reminder*	197
December - *Warm fuzzies*	198

<u>*Concluding Section*</u>

How to Ask the Angels for Their Guidance in Your Life   202

Tools of Light, Gifts from the ALBs

Why I call Them ALB's

Taken from Stop Kickin' My Chair

Before we begin with explanations let me say up front this book is probably devoid of proper sentence structure and contains tons of spelling mistakes, if that bothers you I am sorry. Yet this is me, it is how I speak, it is how I think and how I interact with the world. I am not perfect nor is my work. So forgive my flaws and just get the gist of what I am saying, it is so much more important than the other anyway .

Now as to why I call them ALBs (Angel Like Beings) and not Angels straight out. Mostly because the term/name Angels conjures the ideas of Christian beliefs in ones mind. So since Christianity is considered the mainstream belief system and I am not Christian, I am pagan and I do not follow those beliefs, so came ALBs.

However I do believe in Goddess and God and I serve the Lady and Lord of Light. I believe they have helpers that work within the Lighted path. Those helpers can be called Spirit Guides, Messengers of Faith, Angels or 100 different other things. In the end they are the same, entities on a higher plane who help the Creators spread Positive Loving energy though out the universe. So I decided to call them Angel Like Beings or ALBs for short.

The second reason I call them ALBs is to keep my own ego in check. I don't want to run around sounding all self important saying, "Oh look at me I speak with angels, aren't I important." The term ALBs serves to remind me I am nothing more then a vessel of the Lady and Lord of Light and I work within Their Lighted Loving path. The ALBs are there to guide and help me when I ask and when I am open to their intercessions into my life.

Yes without a doubt I am truly blessed beyond measure to have these beings so close, you could be as well if you allowed them into your life. For those who don't hear or see them as easily as I do I decided to make this book for you. In the back you will see a page that tells you how to **Ask the Angels for Guidance,** try it and look for signs they heard you. I know you will see it and your life will change for the better as you accept and work with these higher beings of unconditional love and support.

Blessings all and may you forever walk within the Lighted positive path
Lady Wolfen Mists

Sept 7th 2004 posted on Delphi
Grid of Living Waters
for healing and anchoring the Light

Dear ones today I learned the most amazing things, so simple really that it seems not real but something all of us probably knows but has never thought of. It has to do with voicing requests to the universe and karma.

First I must set the stage as to how this came to me. I was talking once again with the Angel Like Beings I see and they had came to me and told me how to make **Grid of Living Waters for healing and anchoring the Light.** The information is to be used to help in all forms of healing and in anchoring the much needed Light in these final days of battle against the Darkness that wish to take our free will and remove all positive energies from this dimension and space. Later I will tell you how to get the information, but now let us continue with the lesson I learned from them.

My fear was that if I gave out the instructions on how to do this that the Darkness would take it and pervert it and use it for negative. I was always taught not to give away secrets in the open or your opponent would have the upper hand. The Angel Like Beings smiled at me and said if I had the people ask for the instructions with pure intent and voice (even written, like in an e-mail) that they intended to use these instructions to anchor the Light then it couldn't be used to harm. For in voicing there intentions out to the universe then the universe accepted their actions with positive intent and the results would and could only work with positive results. Even if once the people got it they changed and tried to use it for negative acts, the results for the general population would be positive, as it was given at the request and acceptance for positive use. That only the one who had lied to the universe would reap negative karma as a result of the negativity they wanted to do.

That's all well and good I said but what if in the heart of the user they intend from the beginning to use it for negativity and just said the words to get the information. Again they smiled and answered, just the act of petitioning the Universe for the information, and making voice (or written form) makes a binding intent for the Universe. From this the Universe accepts the intent and that the instructions will be used for positive anchoring and healing thus making an unbreakable bond with the universal energies (God.) This bond cant be changed or broken as the information is delivered on that thought that was accepted by the universe, yet the person has free will and they can change the possibilities of their own results by changing their use once the information has been given.

Beings always determine their own karma and spiritual direction, but for the general population the use will stay as it was first requested for. You see dear Ones, Voiced intentions are powerful binding contractual energies you make with the universe (god) So one must always think before voicing what they want from the universe and be serious to use it as you requested it for.

Once again this seemed to easy to be true but the Angel Like Beings assured me it was so. So I thought about it and said, OK so what if they get the information without having to ask the universe for it. Say they find it or some idiot just starts giving it out to anyone or places it up on the web somewhere. The Angels once more grinned a wide grin and said, because it hadn't been asked for and given from the Universe for use then it simply wouldn't work, that it must be asked for showing the persons intent to use it for good before it would work. The actions in the instructions are important, but the Blessing at the end must be given at the desecration of the universe (God.) If the universe didn't hear the person giving voice (or written form) to pure use for healing and anchoring of the Light it was simply not going to do anything.

But what if someone took the information and devised a way to dedicate a site to the anchoring of the Darkness from it I asked. The Angle like being showing great patience placed an arm about me. He pointed out that like the blessing says, that shadows will always be dispelled by Light and that there is no place of Darkness can not be consecrated and made sacred. Yet there are many places on this world and on other distance planets that places of illuminated Light has been anchored and can never be desecrated by the Darkness no matter what acts happen there. That Light is a symbol for such things as Wisdom, Compassion, Love and Sacred Divine Presence and that there is no where this cant exist or cant win over the Darkness and what it symbolizes. This building and anchoring of the **Grid of Living Waters** is such a place in the physical plane and is to be attempted by only the most dedicated and those most ready to do war against the Darkness.

I was told that those who attempted to build such an anchored space must beware for the dark beings would attack them on any and all levels, as they would want to do as much harm to the soldiers for Light as possible. That such Light Warriors would need to be able to wrap themselves in the cloak of ancient mysteries and Light, of balanced positive energy and universal humility. That they must have few chinks in their armor of Faith and serve with sublime submissiveness to the Lady and Lord of Light (or whatever you call God.) That they must know how to call on other Beings of Light when they were frightened or in crisis, for knowledge is power and be able to accept their help (knowing how to call it great but accepting help is often hard for beginners)

I asked exactly what this **Grid of Living Waters** could be used for and was told to heal all things, as well as make a sacred consecrated space. As space that the Light could flow to and from, and help in the healing of the world on all levels as well as in the accession process of all living beings on this planet to yet another level of enlightenment in our spiritual quest.

So in essence I have learned that no matter what you plan to do with information, how and what you voice its use to the universe for and how the universe accepts that use is how it <u>must be used for the general population</u>. That if you change your voiced use (even if you intended in your heart to use it for something else all together when you asked for it) that is the Karma you will make and will be for you alone and paid to the Universe itself.

So planning to use something for negative when you asked for it for a positive use binds one to a karmic lesson from the universe itself and only affects you the asker, and I would hate to think what a severe and difficult lesson that may be. However if you ask for it for positive use and use it as you asked for it. Then the positive intent for all beings involved that you put out there, will earn you positive karma from the universe, and what a great and glorious lesson that may result in.

As for the **Grid of Living Waters** for healing and anchoring the Light I will be happy to share it with you who ask and who feel ready to use it, if I get the OK from the Angel Like Beings one each of you. I only need an e-mail from you telling me why you want it, how you intend to use it (for positive or negative use). I also need to know if you feel ready to meet the requirements given for a Warrior of the Light. Oh and one last thing just to make me feel better, I would want your word or oath if you will in writing that you will not share this with anyone else without them having to write the same and things as you did. Even better just refer them to me to share this with them.

"We Will Shine the Light into the Darkness and we will create a wondrous place"
LWM

Grid of Living Waters for healing and anchoring the Light Instructions

© Lady Wolfen Mists Sept 7 2004

Please read through this fully once so you get a general idea of what to do **BEFORE** you do it.

Items needed in specific sets of use

Water needed items
- 3 or 9 drops of oxygen supplement like *Aquagen* (can get at any health food store or Silver Hoofs Inc)
- 1/2 gallon Water (Non tap is best but tap can be used if that's all you can get)

Sizing for Stones = Use the size recommended or larger

Small	is dime or smaller
Med	is nickel size quarter
Large	is 50 cent or bigger size

Place In The Ground Stones
- 1 small Black Onyx
- 1 med Angelite
- 1 med to large Quartz Crystal
- 1 small Turquoise
- 1 med Moonstone

Place In Water Stones
- 1 small Ruby or Garnet
- 1 med Amethyst
- 1 small Aventurine Green
- 1 small to med Clear Quartz Crystal
- 1 small Amber (optional)
- 1 small Rose Quartz
- 1 med to Large Angelite

Place in Water Herbs
- 2 pinches of Orange peel (about 1/2 teaspoon)
- 1 pinch of Hyssop (about 1/2 teaspoon)

- 1 palm size of rose petals (about a quarter of a cup)
- -1 palm size of Bay leaf (full leaf is best, about 9 to 13 leafs)

A note to begin with

To use this as a healing well so you can drink from it, it must be a natural spring or not stagnate (moving) pond. If it is not any of these then it is best not to drink the water. If you have a man made spring or pond you can still make it a living water site where you can soak or wash from. Waters from any of these can be added to regular wash cycles, or added to pools or even added to bath or such. In any of the cases this Living water becomes a sacred and consecrated place for all time, no actions no matter how horrendous can undo what you have done in making this a powerful anchored place of the Light, so be sure you want to do this.

Also I must warn you what I was told a word of warning

I was told that those who attempted to build such an anchored space must beware for the dark beings would attack them on any and all levels, as they would want to do as much harm to the soldiers for Light as possible. That such Light Warriors would need to be able to wrap themselves in the cloak of ancient mysteries and Light, of balanced positive energy and universal humility. That they must have few chinks in their armor of Faith and serve with sublime submissiveness to the Lady and Lord of Light (or whatever you call God.) That they must know how to call on other Beings of Light when they were frightened or in crisis, for knowledge is power and be able to accept their help (knowing how to call it great but accepting help is often hard for beginners.) So be sure you are ready for the fight of Light against dark when you attempt to do this. There is NO SHAME in knowing your limits and not being ready to do this work.

My addition to this is that many of you have been picking some, lets just say creepy places to do your grids. This is well and fine and are places that could really do with anchoring the Light but I also want you to practice caution. The Angels **ALWAYS** come in twos so there is no reason you need to do this alone, go in twos (or more) and have someone watch your back while you do this. As for not letting anyone know the instructions you can share the basics with them just don't give them the entire incantation and you will be fine. So be safe while you do this OK?

The Instructions

On day 1

Mix together water and Oxygen supplement (3 or 9 drops I like 9 but that's just my preference.) Place the Aventurine, Ruby or Garnet and Amber in the container of water and oxygen and let "steep" in the sun Light and Moonlight for one full 24 hour (at least more is fine less is not) day.

Day 2 (as the stones steep with the water mixture)

Dig holes to place each individual stone in about 3 to 7 inches down. Place the stones from the ***Place in the ground stones*** section in front of the chosen water site or around it with the water site being the center. However if the chosen water site is deep it is difficult to place the center stone in the center of the grid as it may be many feet under water if you want to use that method. The easiest seems to be to place the stones in front of the chosen water site. Before you ask in front of means in any direction you chose to face with the ground you use in front of the water line.

Now dig the following grid and place the stones as shown

	12:00 **Black Onyx**	
9:00 **Moonstone**	**Center** **Clear Quartz Crystal**	**3:00** **Turquoise**
	6:00 **Angelite**	

Finish placing the stones and cover the stones with dirt

Day 3

Take the steeped water and the rest of the **Place in water stones** out to the well or natural pond or man made pond. Dump the water, oxygen and stone mixture into the chose water site. Then add the Amethyst, Clear Quartz Crystal and the Rose Quartz in the chosen water site. Be sure to leave out the last pieces of Angelite.

Next add herbs from the **Place in the Water Herbs** section, one at a time, no particular order. While doing this ask the Universe (God) something along the lines that this water run with abundance of life healing energy.

The Invocation and Blessing on day 3

Now holding the final item to the chosen water site, which is the Angelite. Say the following or as close as you can (you can have this written down and read it as you hold the Angelite in one hand.

"Gracious Higher Beings of Universal Light,
Bless this place of Life giving water in anchored Light.
Created for a Higher purpose of Living Healing water,
By may actions and thoughts from now to eternity.
Shadows are always dispelled by the Light.
Light Beings of positive, pure divine energies,
so consecrate this section of ground
and all it reaches touches and feeds to and from.
Let this illumination anchor here!
Lighted in positive energies for all eternity and more.
So Mote It Be!"

Now toss the Angelite into the pond on the So Mote it Be!

Final work to close the consecration

For the next seven days (even if it rains or such) leave food and drink (water is fine or fruit juice in a small bowl) for the creatures who visit there. On the 7th day the pond is ready and your sacred ground is created, the Light is anchored and the **Grid of Living Waters for healing and anchoring the Light** has been created.

If it simply impossible for you to be there for 7 days one after another, take 7 days worth of food, in their own containers (like paper bowls or such,) and leave all at once. At home for the 7 days think of being there and seeing the energies steep into the space you have created.

Personal Notes & Experiences

Keepers of Abundance Altar

© LWM 10-20 2004

Items needed

- Altar
- Stone Egg and stand
- White votive
- Writing paper for requests in a special container
- Pens or pencils for writing request in a special container, can be stored with paper
- 2 special Lock boxes with slits
- Sacred Scent Oils
- Flower Scents (i.e. potpourri, rose, jasmine etc.)
- Food or plant leafs
- Pieces of Obsidian in bowl
- Bowl of Holy water or seashells and sand in a bowl
- Sacred Scents incense for smudging
- Plaque

Reason for this tool

This is an altar that must be kept for Life. It is an outside altar in which people (yourself and others) can come and ask for abundance. The altar must be attended by you who becomes High Priest or High Priestess of this sacred space. This will be a permanent fixture in your life. It can be set up on a roadside or a back yard or even a balcony patio situation. Just so the place is outside. The altar itself anchors positive Light to the world, so it can be moved if you move but it MUST be used and set up again if you move to another place. This is not an item you can make or create and go off and leave. It takes attention and tending for the rest of your life so be sure before you create it that you are ready for this responsibility, in case of your death it can be passed on to another but as I said once created it must be continued.

How it works

The universe wishes to give us all abundance, it is the natural order of things. There is nothing in the natural world that works in scarcity the universe created enough of all things for everyone. It is only through social programming and the work ethic that only those who deserve things get them, that we have bought into the idea that there is not enough to go around. This line of thinking has created a self fulfilling prophecy and caused hoarding and greed and stockpiling of what we think are much needed treasures. When the truth is that all things are in abundance and yours for the asking, if those things are in your higher self-interest at the time we "think" we need them. With this in mind the Angel like being have shared with me this altar of abundance where one asks and gives in return (remember balance is needed in all things) to the Goddess and God. Then the universe evaluates the request and acts on it, yet remember no is an answer as well. I personally have found that when my requests are not honored by the universe there is something much better ahead that I had never even dreamed of, I just need to get through the period at hand to reach it.

Anyway each time a request is made to the Universe (Goddess or God) and a sacrifice is given, then the Light is anchored just a little more to this world. The old programmed ideas and notions from society, that keep us from being able to access these truths and treasures on abundance, are torn away and the spiritual world is opened a bit more and life is connected once again to the Higher Powers, as it was meant to be not with the blocks we have created.

This altar in essence creates an open portal that works 24 hours a day, in which energies can pass through in a focused and concentrated manner allowing for the manifestation of Higher Plane work here on Earth. This is all done in Love and Light so there is no need to worry about anything negative using this portal. This is an open portal of Light directly from the Lady and Lord and meant to bestow on Her children the Abundance of Creation that will be in the best interest of our Higher Selves, we only need ask

Instructions

Creation of the actual Altar

First you need to find a spot where the altar can sit for life if possible. A sacred spot where things can grow about it and where you can get to it to tend it easily. Once this is done you need to decide on the type of altar you wish to create. This is key for this will be the piece that is truly sacred and will be used over and over. If you do move this is the piece that will need to be set up in your new place and the work continued from, although the land it sits on is important the actual altar is the truly most sacred thing.

The altar can be made of anything, table wood or stone or such. Just please take into consideration that it must be able to weather the elements year round. I have decided to create this altar in my back yard and will be using one of those Stone benches made of concrete that is often seen in gardens. I plan to sit the altar on a riser to make it taller and this should be perfect for my use. You can make or create whatever works for you.

What you do to tend the altar and to use it

There are several steps to this altar and I would like to lay them out as such, then if needed I will explain them in further detail.

1. The altar once set up will be the receiver of wishes and wants of supplicants. These wishes will be written in symbols that only the supplicant need understand so written word is not necessary, that way the wishes and wants remain private. As the High Priestess or High Priest of the Altar you may also place wishes there for others as well as for the world or dimension.

2. A Balance of energy must be struck on each request. This means a sacrifice must be left. This can be in terms of gifts (monetary or not) What ever the supplicant feels is appropriate. Just so long as it is not Blood or killing of anything. A sacrifice does not take life in any manner it can be flowers or treasures for the Fae, or food or plants or anything like that but nothing that takes life.

3. The request is placed in a special box with a slot (and a lock if you can) and a Stone Egg on a stand, placed upon that box or in front of it. With an unlit white votive in front of all that.

4. The Keeper allows the requests to be upon the altar for 28 days (one full moon cycle) then the box is emptied.

5. Optional addition to placing your wish: Requests for the burning of votive candles to send the supplicants wish to the universe is also made and placed in another locked box. The Keeper will burn the candles for you during the 28 day cycle. Donations for candles are expected to cover the cost of the candle and placed in the box with the requests.

6. The Keeper is expected to wipe the altar with sacred scents each week, patchouli or sandalwood, or frankincense work well. These scents can be wiped about the altar top or on the edges.

7. The Keeper must also layout weekly refreshed symbols of the elements (as weather allows in the winter time)

    Earth = food stuffs or plant
    leafs

    Air = Flower scents like
    potpourri or rose
    scented papers for
    writing requests on

    Fire = Pieces of Obsidian
    placed in a bowl

    Water = Bowl of Holy water
    or Sand and seashells

8. There is a plaque that **MUST** be made, it can be hung above the altar like on a fence or tree or placed on it, or Hung from the front. It can even be painted upon the table top of the altar itself. Practically anyplace and anyway you want to put it within a 10 foot range. It **must say the following**

    "Angels of Abundance hear the hearts desires stored here
    Lift them up and hold them near
    Bless these people and this space
    Anchor the Light of abundance to this place"

The following is the layout for the items; Please notice the plaque is not included in this layout as I am not sure where you wish to place it, but don't FORGET it as it is extremely important without it nothing will work well.

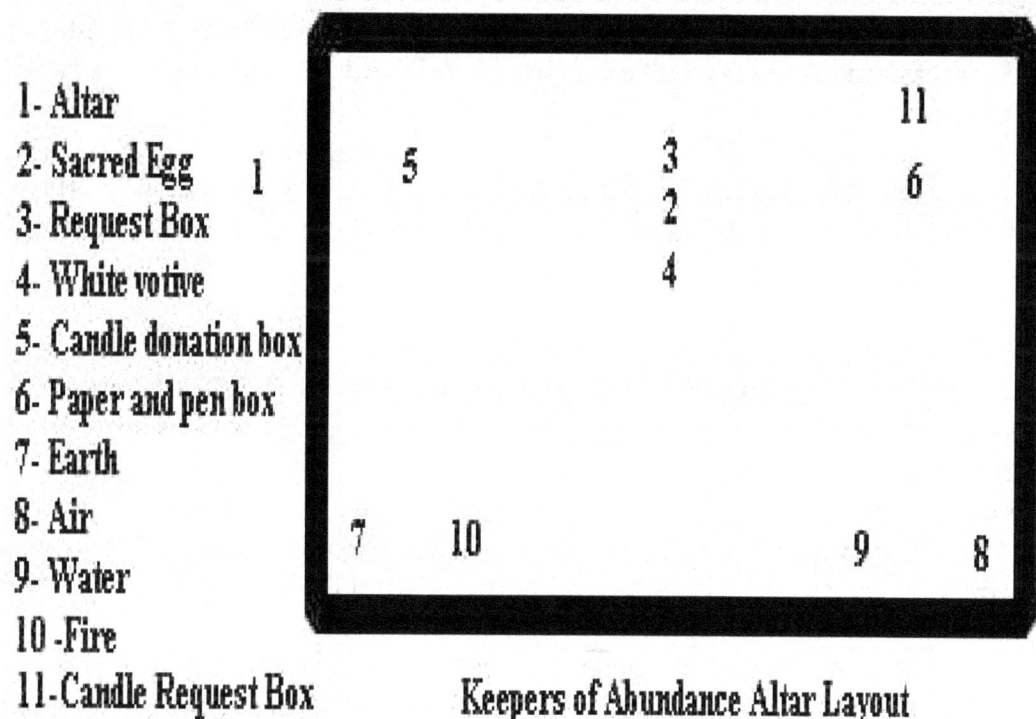

1- Altar
2- Sacred Egg
3- Request Box
4- White votive
5- Candle donation box
6- Paper and pen box
7- Earth
8- Air
9- Water
10- Fire
11- Candle Request Box

Keepers of Abundance Altar Layout

Further explanation of items.

In the number One I speak of writing in symbols, this is anything that means or exemplifies to the supplicant what it is that they are asking for, The Keeper need not make sense of it. The only need is that the supplicant puts their energy into the "written request" so that the universe can decipher what it is. That they send out their thoughts to the universe as they request what they wish for. All requests do not need to be material in nature and can be for such things as healing, safety and peace .

In number two I speak of balance being struck. This means a sacrifice left, in the olden days such sacrifices were used by the High Priest and High Priestess of the temple to live on. It is payment not only to the Goddess and God for their loving energies but for the High Priestess or High Priest who tend this altar.

Now some may take issue with this, I have nothing more to say on it. It's what the Angel Like Beings told me, and if they feel such payments can be used by the Keepers who are we to argue. It shows respect to the Keepers who have dedicated their lives to this work as well as to the universe to show your appreciation of the gifts you receive. Gifting of items is fine as well as giving of food stuffs to the animals who live outside as well.

Oh and the gifts can be laid on the alter if small enough or on another designated bench or space or placed on the ground around the altar (like food stuff for the critters)

In number three I speak of a special box with a slot to place requests, this is self explanatory. The Egg and stand may need some explaining, it is a symbol of spirit and because of the egg shape without edges or corners the energy is constantly moving and self renewing. It never really needs cleansed and works 24/7. A perfect vehicle to focus the energies of request and send them to the universe. The stand is to place the egg upon. The white votive that remains not lit is a symbol of Light in the Darkness and the concentrated energies of the Keeper who works to tend this altar and to anchor the Lighted path to it.

Number four speaks of the cycle in which the requests are sent out, this is one moon phase. It can go to 1 calendar month if the Keeper sees fit (31 days) but not less than 28.

Number five speaks of requests for burning a candle and box for candle donations. This is an **additional extra** that the Keeper can do for you if you like. You need only write your request down (in written word not symbols) like "please Light a candle for bobs healing, or Please grant me financial abundance or please anchor the

Light securely here." Then place it in the box, the keeper will Light the additional focused and concentrated energies for you and burn your candle. Donations should run about 50 cents to $1.00 per request. This helps pay for the upkeep of the altar and the items need for its care as well as the supplies.

In number six we talk about upkeep of the altar itself, this is to be done weekly as weather allows for it. Don't be trudging through the snow to do this and risk your life, be reasonable. Also if there is an awful storm coming the Keeper can remove the items and replace them when the storm passes or the snow has been dug away. Can you tell I live in North Dakota and snow is an issue here, but this goes for rain and such as well. Remember you are the Keeper and it is up to you to tend the altar to the best of your ability so do what you think is best.

Number seven speaks of placement of items to represent the elements, these can be used again and again. It states they must be refreshed this is easy to do, weekly just run them through the smoke of a sacred scent such as sandalwood, blue roses, sage or some such scent, 3 times right to left. Just so you know this is called smudging. This removes any mis aligned energies from everyday life and refreshes your items for the new week. You can also use scents that correspond to the closet Sabbat (if you are Wiccan) or a seasonal scent. Please note that in winter you can use food stuff for Earth instead of fresh leafs. However pine looks great there in the winter as well.

As for Water because of the possibility of freeze you can use sand and seashells to represent water so the holy water won't freeze. A recipe for Metaphysically correct holy water is included at end of instructions

Lastly but most importantly number eight tells of **the plaque that must be made**. These are the **words of power that activate the actual altar and must be used**. They can be mounted on, in around the altar in any manner you like. I think I will be painting mine on a wood piece and the putting a coating of polyurethane on it so it won't rub off. I will also add other pretty painted decorations to it and then place it under my Egg and stand. I think it should work very well. You of course can use any creative idea you may have. Just be sure to do it or the altar won't be activated.

Things that may come up

What to do if some one places blood on your altar or desecrates it in some manner?

Just clean it up. Smudge it with sacred incense real good and wipe it down with the sacred scent oils mentioned above. Like all the other angel tools this cant be "ruined"

as the Light is already anchored to the tool (in this case the altar) and is working no matter what! So don't let it stop what you are doing.

What if my altar gets old and breaks?

This is another issue that may come up, especially with outside wood altars that aren't properly protected from the elements. Just take s piece of the old altar and place it on the new altar for 28 days (one moon cycle) so it may endow the new altar with its energies and then the new altar is ready to go. You can use the new altar as the old one transfers energies to it as well.

Some people may wish to keep a part of the old original altar on the new one or even under it, that's fine or you can get rid of it as you see fit. Placing it along side of those buried (including animals) helps to keep that space sacred and anchored in the Light as well. Like the altar does in abundance work, here it opens a constant portal to the Goddess and God and things can pass through easily and in love and Light.

Well I hope I haven't left anything out, if I have I'm sure I will hear the question from one of you and them I will add an appendix (hee hee) With that said that's all there is to building the Keepers of Abundance Altar. I hope you use it with the love it was intended and I hope you become wondrously abundant in all things positive.

Blessings,
May You Always Walk Within The Light
Lady Wolfen Mists

Personal Notes & Experiences

Open Healing Channel tool

Sept 10, 2004

OK once again the Angels have been sharing with me....This time it is for Healers and those who wish to help heal the World in General. It is a tool called **Open Healing Channel** It has two parts to it, a tool for general world healing that opens a clear focused channel of healing Light as well as a more personal use to healers which helps in the healing of specific people/beings in a "hands on if you will" type of way.

It also meshes well with Faith Healers, Reiki Practitioners, Animal Healers, Magnet Therapists and most any healers of almost all walks and paths who have a sincere wish to help and reach out to other being in pain.

This tool is used to open a solid healing channel for healers as well as continuous healing energies for the World. The healing channel helps to anchor Light filled energies directly from the Universe. Yet its main purpose is to focus the healing energies and Creation energies of the Universe (flowing directly from Goddess and God) to help in healing all things it touches. As well as opening the Chakras of all living things and teaching total acceptance of these loving healing energies.

Like before I was afraid that such a tool with so much in possibilities could be twisted and perverted to do unthinkable harm in the wrong hands. Again the Angels, always patient and caring with me, assured me that this tool must be asked for as were the **Grid of Living Waters** and that the voiced request when asked was all that counted. That in sharing these instructions the universe would only accept and approve those requests that would be of Higher positive use and intent and it didn't matter what was done to pervert it, it simply would not work.

So once more if you, as a healer, are interested e-mail me. Give me a day or so to type up the instructions, as I just got the information myself and these a bit to wade through. I caution you again: Like before you must consider if you are advanced enough to use this spiritually. The spirits of the dark forces are not gonna just let you do this without some repercussions, so be ready to have negative obstacles placed in your path to turn you from this work.

With all that said if you feel you are one of the Chosen to do this I will be happy to share it with you who ask and who feel ready to use it, if I get the OK from the Angel Like Beings one each of you. I only need a e-mail from you telling me why you want it, how you intend to use it (for positive or negative use). I also need to know if you feel ready to meet the requirements given for a Healer .

I will also request your word or oath in writing that you will not share this with anyone else without them having to write the same and things as you did. Even better just refer them to me to share this with them. Feel free to let others know that this tool or the other is available, just have them e-mail me the same information.

So now I go off to type up the instructions, and wish you all Blessings and a wonderful Light filled abundant day. Also take a moment or two to send loving healing thoughts to the friends and families of those who lost loved ones in 911 in 2001, the pain of these people is still raw and fresh and they deserve all our love, understanding and healing energies we can send.

Blessings,
LWM

Open a Healing Channel Tool Instructions

© LWM 9-9 2004

Items needed:

For Session or Personal use
Frankincense Oil
Myrrh Oil

Stones for use in Pyramid Tool
Jet or moss agate
White Quartz or Sodalite
Labradorite or Spectrolite
Citrine
Selenite (with a point is best)
Charolite (is best) or Amethyst (substitute)

Other items for building and Use within the Pyramid tool
-2 large size Jump rings (*The little round loops used to attach pendants and such to necklaces*)
-1 Jewelry finding bail (easy to glue on stone) *a bail is a loop that is glued to stone or such to make a pendant.*
-1 1inch to 2 inch chain
-Glue to glue bail to stone
-8 pipe cleaners 16 inches long (any color)

In selecting jump rings one needs to be small enough to fit the chain link and attach to the pipe cleaner, the other needs to be small enough to attach to the pipe cleaner and the bail you select to glue your stone to.

Selecting a bail. There are lots of bails you can us I have just given you an idea of two of the easiest and mot popular. The one is a fold over leaf kind that is easily glued to the stone. The other is a simple eye bail, you can either get these flat on the bottom or with a screw eye and remove the screw eye pin with cutting pliers and glue it securely to the stone.

Glues to use I like a special glue we use with stones called *Bond 527* it can be picked up at any hobby store, or you can try supper glue (which doesn't always hold as well when a stone had a finish)

Reason for this tool

This tool is used to open a solid healing channel for healers as well as continuous healing energies for the World. The healing channel helps to anchor Light filled energies directly from the Universe. Yet its main purpose is to focus the healing energies and Creation energies of the Universe (flowing directly from Goddess and God) to help in healing all things it touches. As well as opening the Chakras of all living things and teaching total acceptance of these loving healing energies.

Instructions

First day

First you need to take the bail you have chosen for the selenite stone and attach it to the end that wont be pointing down. The end with the point or focused end will be the point from which the energy will flow, and we want as little blockage there as possible. To attach the chosen bail just glue it and let it sit to dry, remember with many glues less is more.

Once this has dried sufficiently take the chain and add jump rings to both ends sit aside as the stone completes it drying stage for at least 24 hours to get a good set.

Take all the stones and place them in the moonlight overnight while the bail is drying, this cleanses them and powers them up for later.

Second day

Now since this is going to be a portable and easy to assemble tool we will build it with pipe cleaners, which are malleable and easy to use. Yet if you want something more solid and sturdy you can use something like copper tubing, which conducts energies easily and makes a giant circuit. Just be sure its at least 12 inches tall or higher, but not much smaller.

OK now moving on, connect your pipe cleaners so that they are approx. 16 inches long. You will need 8 of these. Once you have these you begin to build a four sided pyramid.

The base will be approx. 14 inches per side, allowing for 1 inch per end to twist and connect the pipe cleaners.

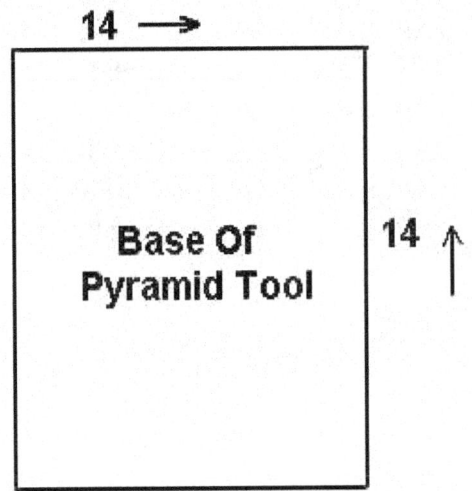

Next make the pyramid top slant at an approx. 45 degree angle. Its easier to make the top first then connect to the base. Again allowing for 1 inch per end to connect. Also at the top inside of the pyramid make a loop, this will be used to connect the bigger jump ring and allow the Selenite to hang from it.

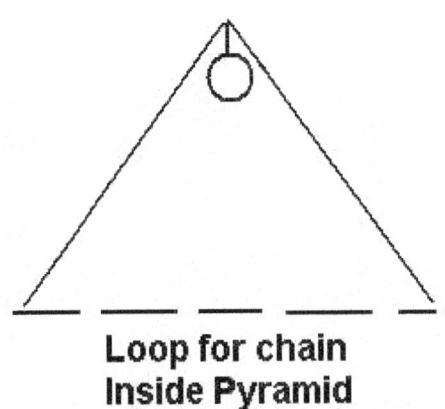

Loop for chain Inside Pyramid

Once the above is complete attach the chain to the selenite pendant (which should be dry by now) and jump ring to the loop made inside the top of the Pyramid. Connect the top part of the pyramid to the base. Starting at the right top corner and working around it like the figure shows below.

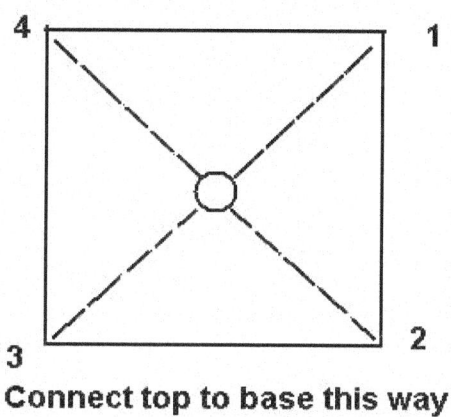

Connect top to base this way

That's all there is to building the pyramid which will act as an Open healing channel for you.

To Use the Tool

To use the pyramid you will need to find a place to sit it that allows it to work without interruptions, as it opens a focused and easy flowing healing channel to all things the energies touch.

Let's say you place it on a table or shelf. You will need to place the stones inside the points of the pyramid, in the following manner.

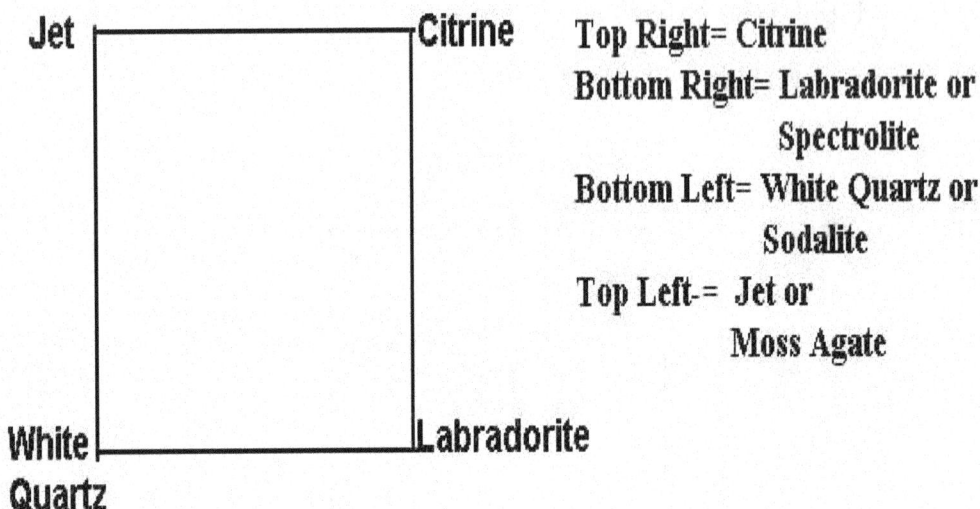

Key to Layout

Once the stones are in place say the following:

"Healing Energies of Light as I placed these stones ,
I consciously and with pure intent open a flowing healing Channel.
Through which many focused and concentrated Light energies flow in a continuous stream to this plane.
From this given tool may there flow all the loving and Healing Creation energies available in the universe.
Making for the better all that it touches, spirit, body, mind, flesh and non,
All of Creation will feel and respond to this positive open healing channel"

Let the tool work for as long as you like (24/7) or you can close it down at any given time by removing the 4 stones inside the pyramid. Each time you reopen the channel you will need to say something to the universe like what is written above.

To use the Tool to strengthen a healers ability in a session

Do all of the above but place the Charolite or Amethyst under the hanging selenite in the center of the pyramid.

Next place a dab of Frankincense oil in the middle of the left palm and a dab of Myrrh Oil in the middle of the right palm.

Now reach in and pick up the Charolite stone (or amethyst). Hold the stone in between both hands, so the frankincense and Myrrh touch the stone, (actually your hands should be cupped palm to palm holding the stone so it looks like you are praying.) Breath gently through your mouth, blow that breath onto your prayer like positioned hands. Do this 3 times, then place hands inside the pyramid.

Breathing regularly, but with eyes closed so you can really feel the sensations in your hand, count to 7. Then blow out through your mouth. Do this action 3 times then on the final 3rd time take your hands out of the pyramid. Place the stone you were holding (Charolite or Amethyst) under the hanging Selenite once more.

You now have opened a connection of focused healing energy through you in which the energies automatically know where to go and what to do to "jump start" the natural healing of the person in need. There is no need for the practitioner to have a understanding of the obstacles or even try to figure out where and why the blockages and obstacles occurred, simply let the universe do what it does best in returning the balance needed on all levels. These energies will flow in a powerful manner much like turning on a faucet. This is fully effective for about 45-60 minutes and then you must do it again.

Notes of Interest

- This is great to use with Reiki Practitioners, Faith Healers and anyone who has "hands on healing skills" It aids not only in successful healing energies , being able to remove and dislodge any obstacles and blockages but for the total acceptance of the energies by the person being healed.

- You may notice your hands getting warmer or turning red or even a buzz, this is OK. It just shows the channel is open and moving energies through you as well as the tool, If it becomes to much to take you can always rinse your hands with water, it will not stop the energy that is working.

- Drinks and food may be energized as well with this tool. Just place the food (plate) or drink inside the activated pyramid for about the space of 9 heartbeats. This will aid in delivering healing energies through food or drink intake. These energies stay active for about 20-25 minutes before consumption after that they need to be powered up again.

Blessings,
May You Always Walk Within The Light
Lady Wolfen Mists

Personal Notes & Experiences

Spirit Shield Wreath

OK so like I said I have new tool from the Angel Like Beings that has to do with protection.

Like all the other tools before I can share this with you I need e-mail from you on your positive use intent and that you will only use it in the highest good of all concerned. You will not share it with others unless they too submit an e-mail or letter that shows their intent is to only use it for positive and for the highest good of everyone.

I really feel this will be a powerful tool that can be used by many followers of the Lighted path so if your interested just let me know.

Reason for this tool

This tool was given to me by the Angel Like Beings to be used in a constant setting. It is easy to make and will send out focused and concentrated Light energy. It will battle the Darkness and allow for you to choose specific targets you may wish to protect.

Blessings,
LWM

Spirit Shield Wreath Instructions

© Lady Wolfen Mists April 11 2005

Items needed
- Wreath Base
- Hot Glue Gun or Wire to secure items to wreath
- Wire cutter If you use wire
- Floral picks if you use them to glue item to
- Programmed Quartz Crystal
- Other Stones of Protection
- Herbs of Protection
- Symbols of the Light that you like
- Sacred incense of your choice- for example sandalwood, frankincense, blue roses or what you may like)

Reason for this tool

This tool was given to me by the Angel Like Beings to be used in a constant setting. It is easy to make and will send out focused and concentrated Light energy. It will battle the Darkness and allow for you to choose specific targets you may wish to protect.

How it works

This wreath uses the concentrated and focused combined physical, emotional and spiritual energies that it was imbued with upon its creation to continually send out a protective shield for who or what ever. Size really doesn't matter and you can have as many of these as you wish. For example you could have one to protect the world and one for innocents in general and one for your kids or loved ones or yourself. As many as you want to make hung all around your home, school or office. Because of the shape it is self cleansing. Depending on where it is placed (in moonlight or not) it may need re-powered every now and then.

Instructions on creating the Wreath

So how do you do it, well you do have to be a little crafty but its not hard. 1st get a wreath, the one they showed me was just a common floral wreath that had rose buds and other fake flowers in it. The flowers can be fake or they can be dried, its up to you. The actual wreath itself can be any type even the fake pine wreaths of Yule or Grape wreaths. Anything that is circular and that you can add things to.

Next begin adding the things you want to empower your wreath with. flowers, herbs, stones and symbols of the Lighted path (like angels or even a small sword or things like that.) I plan to paint my Angel and even get a pewter sword that you can get from those hobby stores that sell pewter figurines for role playing games. They may have lots of symbols and even pewter angels I can customize and add to my wreath to empower it.

If you are choosing herbs you may want to make a combined sachet of herbs and place them in fifty cent or bigger size lace circles that can be gathered up as bags with a ribbon to hang from your wreath. It can be any combination you like, but I HIGHLY suggest you <u>add OAK, CEDAR, SANDALWOOD, FRANKINCENSE TEARS and HOLLY if you can.</u> It need not be fresh, dried is OK. I have included a list of possible herbs that have been traditionally used for protection, it is by no means exhaustive, just a guide to get you started. Any combination of these Herbs will help.

In choosing to add Stones you will NEED 1 programmed crystal to act as a conduit of energy. This you can either program yourself if you are VERY good at this. It is imperative that this crystals programming not be one that can be misused or "twisted" or broken. If you cant do this get a hold of me and I can program such a crystal for you at reasonable costs.

Stones can be hot glued onto the wreath in any pattern you like. I have even bought those picks you can get in the fake flower section and glued stones to the leaves on the pick and then interwoven the pick into the wreath or into floral foam (that smushy green blocks you can get at just about any craft store.) I inserted it into open areas of my wreath, and fill in as I like. As I said it can be any combination you like, but I HIGHLY suggest you add Black Obsidian, Mahogany Obsidian, Gold goldstone, Purple goldstone, Gaia stone (if doing Earth Work) and Angelite if you can get it. I have also included a list of stones that have been traditionally used over the years for protection, it is by no means exhaustive, just a guide to get you started.

Then there is the use of color, you can use anything that you feel drawn to that would be protective, some of the colors I like are all shades of purple as well as iridescent white, all shades of green, gold and silver color work well. **Avoid red and black** as these colors can easily be distorted as to meanings and can be used in negative manners if one isn't an expert in this area and ward making.

Begin making your wreath, **just be sure to leave a space in the very center to attach your main symbol and at the bottom center of the circle to place your crystal**. Point up towards the main symbol. This is better explained later. In the meantime place anything else where ever you feel moved to allowing it to come together as you desire. Enjoy what you are doing as there is no way of doing this wrong. Be sure that you concentrate your energies on the person, place or thing you wish to shield from the negative energies out there. See this shield as impenetrable and unbreakable. When you have added everything you want and all is done

As you build your personal wreath be sure to have a picture or symbol of the person place or thing you wish to create. For example in mine I will place a picture of the planet Earth as I wish to protect the word, so it will be mounted in the center of the wreath. . You **MUST place the picture or symbol in the center**. If you have problems making sure this stays in place you can attach it to a pick and place the pick into the wreath. A pick is anything that has a wire or wood sick that can be secured to the wreath. Just glue the item to the pick and use the pick to secure it. The same with the programmed crystal. Rather than try to explain this just see the figure below for an example. Please note this is just to show you what to do, it is not actual wreaths that have been used for this tool

Above figure shows Placement of **MUST items** in a traditional Wreath

The ritual of Consecration

Once you have constructed the entire wreath and cleaned up your mess, you must now consecrate it to the Light and allow it to become a tool to be used for all eternity.

All you need do is to take your wreath and place it in the moonlight, be sure you know North, East, South , West. If possible outside is a wonderful feeling, if not just allow the moonlight to touch you. The phase of the moon does not matter.

Light your sacred scent and allow it to burn. Lift your Wreath and allow the smoke from the incense to flow over (smudge) your completed wreath. Facing the East say the following;

Watchers of the East, Keepers of this element and Guardians of air, I implore you to accept this tool I have made and Bless it to be a tool of the Light. Let it send out constant energy to protect those who it was intended for and let it anchor the Light in this world, realm and dimension. Let me be the Warrior you can use and let me make fast my spirit to the Light and to the tools I use and create. Come stand beside me and work with me so that together what we intend and what we create will be in the most positive interest of all creation in all dimensions and realms and kingdoms that exist, have existed and are yet to be.

Wait 7 heartbeats and then turn to the South and say.

Watchers of the South, Keepers of this element and Guardians of fire, I implore you to accept this tool I have made and Bless it to be a tool of the Light. Let it send out constant energy to protect those who it was intended for and let it anchor the Light in this world, realm and dimension. Let me be the Warrior you can use and let me make fast my spirit to the Light and to the tools I use and create. Come stand beside me and work with me so that together what we intend and what we create will be in the most positive interest of all creation in all dimensions and

realms and kingdoms that exist, have existed and are yet to be.

Wait 7 heartbeats and then turn to the West and say.

Watchers of the West, Keepers of this element and Guardians of water, I implore you to accept this tool I have made and Bless it to be a tool of the Light. Let it send out constant energy to protect those who it was intended for and let it anchor the Light in this world, realm and dimension. Let me be the Warrior you can use and let me make fast my spirit to the Light and to the tools I use and create. Come stand beside me and work with me so that together what we intend and what we create will be in the most positive interest of all creation in all dimensions and realms and kingdoms that exist, have existed and are yet to be.

Wait 7 heartbeats and then turn to the North and say.

Watchers of the North, Keepers of this element and Guardians of earth, I implore you to accept this tool I have made and Bless it to be a tool of the Light. Let it send out constant energy to protect those who it was intended for and let it anchor the Light in this world, realm and dimension. Let me be the Warrior you can use and let me make fast my spirit to the Light and to the tools I use and create. Come stand beside me and work with me so that together what we intend and what we create will be in the most positive interest of all creation in all dimensions and realms and kingdoms that exist, have existed and are yet to be.

Wait 7 heartbeats and then look up and say the following (if you are a follower of the Lady and Lord say Lady as well as Lord, if you follow only a Lord substitute just Lord. If you have no gender for your idea of creator then just substitute Creative Spirit or Great spirit what ever works for you.)

Most Blessed Lady and Lord of Light I come before you a child, wanting to serve you all the days of my life. I offer to you this meager working tool and ask for your activation of it and your powerful energy to flow through it. (you may feel a surge of energy as the Universe activates your tool) Allow me to act in your name as a warrior for the Lighted path, grant me wisdom and knowledge, compassion and Love as

well as the ability for justice and to protect those in need. Keep my heart and work pure and my intent focused. Keep the Angels at my side and my ego forever in check as I serve you with a loving humble heart. Please most loving Lady and Lord let the moonlight cleanse and repower this tool and may it never be desecrated or corrupted.

Now turn once more to the incense and pass it through the smoke, allowing the smoke to set the intentions, words and feelings into the new tool.. Wait another 7 heart beats and that's it. You can let the incense burn out if you wish or put it out its up to you.

You may hang your wreath up right away if you like or wait until the next day it doesn't matter. If you place it outside or in a window where it gets continues moonlight you really don't have to repower it often. If it spends time inside like an room (for a child) or an office or something like that then you will need to repower it now and again. Once a month is good. You can do this through the use of an oil I make from a variation of the Angel Powder tool. Just a drop or two and it repowers things right up. This is also good if there seems to be a constant onslaught against the person, place or thing you are trying to protect. It also helps if the energies around the wreath seems a bit "out of whack" and the flow feels uneven. Such a feeling can be a sign that your tool has been identified by the Darkness and is under constant attack to break or crack what it is doing. You may need to up the positive energies here and reaffirm that this is a tool to be used by the Light.

Cleansing & Re-powering the tool

If you don't have the oil you can try to re-power it by moonlight but there are no guarantees this will work for wreaths that are not exposed to he moonlight 24 hours a day. Extreme bursts of such energies my be to much for the tool to hand and having all those stones, herbs and symbols all cleansing at once could be much like putting the jumper cables on a battery backwards. It will all just blow up and explode. I highly recommend the use of the Angel oil, just to have it on hand. It help makes the cleansing and re-powering smoother .

OK so that's about it. Blessing you in its use! Please keep me posted on how it works for you. I really find these Angel tools fascinating they seem so simple but work so very well and use so many things form the Earth. I wonder why we did not think of them by ourselves. Ahhh but I guess that is what divine guidance is for ☺

Blessings,May You Always Walk Within The Light
Lady Wolfen Mists

Personal Notes & Experiences

Nov 07 2008
Chest Guard Tool

I find myself once more in my chair floating along, I have been here before and I am relaxing and comfortable. I realize that it seems when I hurt the worst on the physical world I often find myself in this place. Looking around I see others floating by, some seem to be swimming others just flying or floating as I am. I see a few souls I recognize as being there before when I was, they wave and I wave back.

Then I hear the sound of hoofs and I wonder where it comes from. It sounds like 2 horses running full gallop coming closer but I see nothing. I keep looking in the direction I hear them and I see a small Light coming at me. Closer and closer comes the Light and soon I see it is a rider on a horse and right beside them is another horse. A catch in my throat, dare I hope. Could it be? I love ridding and I don't get to do it at all in the physical anymore. Maybe it is my darling spirited Teyman Anemos.

Closer now they are and Lights flash off these horses their whiteness so brilliant they seem almost blue. Their black saddles contrasts greatly against the flashes of Light as the Light hits the silver embellishments and glitters and shimmers into my eyes.

The rider is large and strong. He is in battle armor, which gleams with polished metal that seems to move with his every movement as if it is almost alive. The front of his chest sports a chest guard that is Silver in color and shows a Light that is brighter then anything around us. Stones deck the front of the chest guard and the design they make seems a powerful grid.

The face is aquiline and I know right away it is so. They pull up right beside me and he looks down at me and removes his helmet, His wings spread wide and they are white with very very black tips.

"Michael, you look magnificent sitting up there!" He grins and says, "And so will you, Do you want to ride for awhile or would you rather just sit here in that ol' chair and relax?"

"Oh no I suppose I can ride, I wouldn't want you to feel alone in this," I reply laughingly. Teyman is now hitting my chair with her head, much like when Michael kicks it. "Hey Stop hitting my chair Tey, I'm getting up, I'm getting up. You are teaching her bad things Michael, She's kicking my chair like you do!"

Michael has a hardy laugh and I mount Tey. She flips her head into the air and snorts. I am excited to let her have the lead. Yet I also notice a sound it is small right now, kinds a hum and it seems to be very soft but there is no missing it. I cock my head trying to listen for it, to see where it comes from but I am interrupted by a voice.

"Come on, I'll race ya! Winner gets lunch for the other!" Off she goes.

"Hey that's cheating, you took off to soon." I am racing to catch up but it is really no race. Tey's stride is long and steady and she catches up without breaking a sweat. Se rides beside without a problem and holds her own, like the wind she is.

While riding beside Michael I can see the Chest guard even better it is amazing to say the least, to be honest I just don't have words for how magnificent it is. I ask about it. "Michael why so much armor and why all the stones on the chest guard?"

"Oh things here have been a bit up in the air if you will," he grins and chuckles at making a joke. "So much happening around us and we must always be ready and never caught unawares. Right now for who knows how long this is our daily uniform, work armor. The stones sit up a power grid. I will explain later when you are getting lunch," and he kicks his horse and begins to pull away.

"Oh no you don't!" I yell and I whisper in Tey's ear. "Run baby, run hard and beat that scoundrel" Off she goes like that was all she was waiting for and soon I am far ahead of Michael with him eating my star dust!!!!

Michael finally shows up a few minutes later I am already settled in the Angel Lounge and drinking a soda, no one else is there but the kitchen crew and they are behind the counter. Tey has been turned over to handlers at the stable and will receive only the best of care.

Michael comes in wiping his face from sweat; his wings are darker then normal. He is grumbling above it not being fair I have the south wind and he has Zepyhrus. Everyone knows the west never blows as fast as the south.

I Laugh "Gezz are you a sore loser or what." He looks at me with dark eyes. "Of course I am a sore loser, I'm a solider I **have** to win. But I do live up to my word, so what can I get you for lunch."

"Oh don't worry about it, I felt sorry for your pitiful riding abilities and ordered. All you need to do is get your own stuff. They will bring my chicken and fries soon."

"Pitiful riding abilities, I'll have you know I have ridden for thousands of years before you were born"

"Well then that's even more pitiful to have me beat ya!" He looks cross and stares at me for a few minutes, then a smile creeps up his face. It grows to a gleaming grin and then a belly laugh.

"That's so true cub, it doesn't say much for me at all does it, we will have to ride more often. At least let me get you some more to eat while we wait."

He grabs my glass and goes to order his lunch and refill my soda. He returns and flings himself in to the chair across the table. His helmet has long been thrown onto the table when he was having his hissy fit on losing and I notice once more his wings are white. He reaches over and releases the buckles on the side that hold the Chest guard on.

"I'm gonna loosen this while I sit here, you aren't gonna try and stab me are you?" "Not unless you give me a reason to," I say holding up my butter knife. He grins and shakes his head. Once more I hear the low hum I heard earlier but its just out of my hearing range and I wonder if I am imagining it all.

"OK," I say "You said you would tell me about the grid on the chest armor thing."

"It's a chest guard and the stones are set in a specific configuration that gives protection as well as power to the wearer. Then it enhances natural abilities as well as adding wisdom, compassion and balancing striking energy with it all?"

"Striking energy?"

"Ummm lets see, the ability to fight and end the essence of another and to send that negative energy back to the pool of energy the universe creates from. The universe absorbs that energy and creates something more positive from it all"

"OK I get it, it helps you know when to kill something and send it back where it came from so it can be used in a more positive way?"

"Yea that's pretty much it. When you're a Spirit Warrior you must always watch your balance and your wisdom, compassion. Keeping it all equalized so that you don't kill just because you can. That would place you over the line and just as bad as the Darkness. If you can see some Light in the being then we don't want to end its essence.

They have a chance of changing for the better, but if it becomes you or them, or if it is so dark there isn't even a speck of Light left it could be best that it is released to start over in creation. These are some of the tasks a Spirit Warrior must face daily.

Anyway this chest guard kinda acts like a super computer but here on the etheric planes and keeps us appraised of what's what and keeps us as protected as we can be. It is a tool of the children of the Light."

Our food had arrived and we both began to eat. "But I can see it so why cant the Darkness see it and make one to?" I asked.

Taking a bite of his roast beef sandwich and dipping a fry in ketchup he said, "Oh that's an easy one, its no secret. Even if they did make one it would destroy them just to wear it. The stones increase Light levels by like a trillion percent. If the dark filled entities were to come in contact with this grid it would simply end their existence or lift their frequency so much they would no longer be stuck in the pits of the dark. Ya know like when you were in the pits of Darkness and saw those who were so beaten down they couldn't even reach up. Well wearing a tool like this would not only let them reach up but they would break though and fill with Light, if they so desired to. So I am all for them knowing about it and making their own."

"Could I make one to wear Michael?

"Sure I don't see why not, you're a spirit Warrior, if you think it would help I don't think there's any reason you couldn't have it or anyone else who would want to have one."

"Does it have to be on metal? Can it be on material or wood or something like that?

"Well it can be anything you want to put it on to wear. It's the stones and the griding that matters."

"What about the size of the stones, any specific size? What is the stone layout."

No any size works, it's the qualities of the stone that the universe taps into not the size. It doesn't matter if it's tumbled; raw or cut it just matters its that kinda stone. The layout..." he reaches for the chest guard.

"Well here look for yourself. I'm hungry." He lays the chest guard on the table and I sketch it down. Michael tears into his 3rd sandwich and my left over fries. I am not very hungry I am more interested in this Chest Guard Tool I think it will help a lot of people out there who are working in the Light and who are awakening. It fascinates me.

He takes a drink and says, "Oh before I forget the Rubies at the top, those are mine. My stone ya know, everyone has one they like best or several they connect with. You don't have to have them for the tool I just added them to mark it as my armor. You can always place what you like best there if you want or some place the stones of their generals there so we know what squad you belong to. I think for you humans you would want to add one or two of your own special stones and maybe something that connects you to the Lady and Lord of Light. Just my suggestion though you don't have to do it."

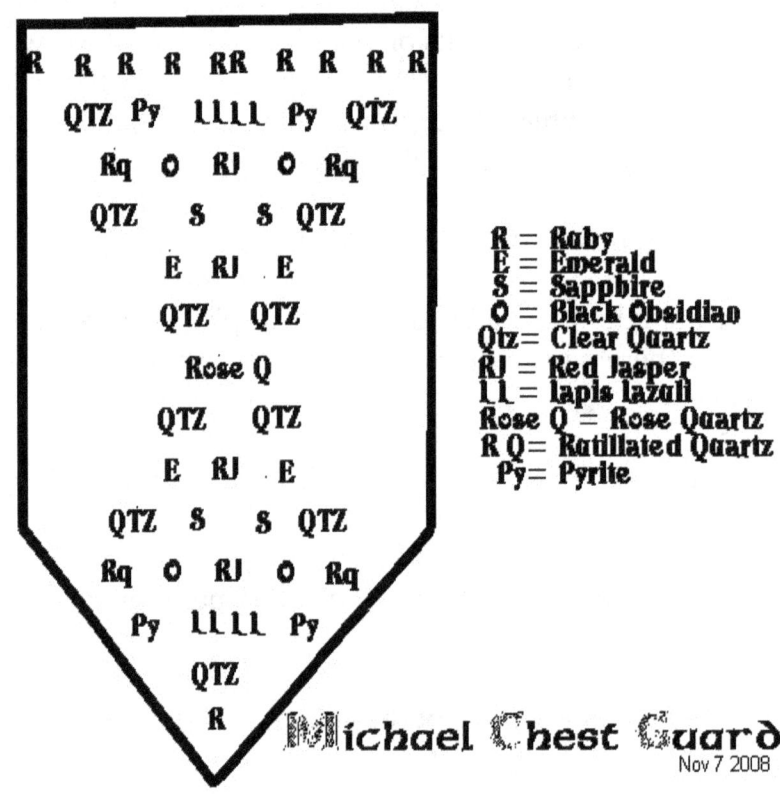

"This is so neat Michael, I will try and make something like this. Thanks for showing it to me. "

The door opens and in walks 6 or so other ALBs, they too are in working uniforms. Four are in full dress armor and two in work medical robes with a solar cross on the front of the robes, I have never seen these robes before. The healers have a large piece of Rose Quartz in the center or their robes with stone points coming away from the Rose Quartz. All is encircled with what looks like Fancy Jasper on one and Aventurine on the other. I ask what they are, Michael tells me these are marks of healers and these are like the chest guard but helps healers do their job. They heal on many levels including healing the sick and tortured minds and souls of those enslaved to the Darkness. Wow I think that takes a really special person.

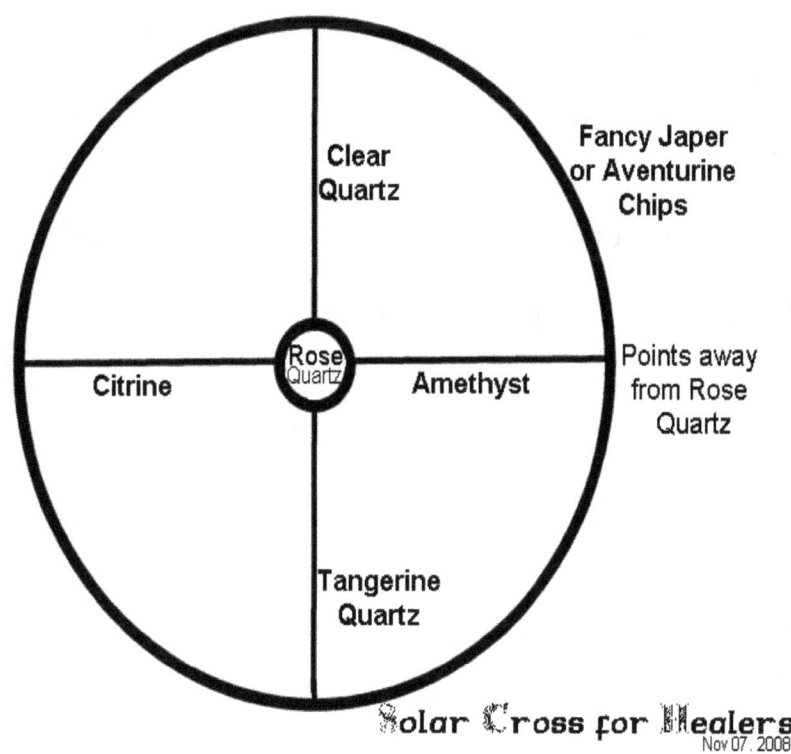

Solar Cross for Healers
Nov 07, 2008

As I sit there I begin to be aware of the humming sound I heard before only this time it's stronger and louder. The hum is amazing it seems to emanate from the very walls but not. It's everywhere and no where and as the hall fills with other ALBs it gets louder and louder.

There are several standing in line to get food and I realize what it is. They are talking and laughing and just being normal but their wings, their wings are vibrating. They seem to be phasing in and out and as they do they hum. A wonderful warming hum that is low but grows as they congregate together.

I ask Michael about it, what is it and why is it happening. He explains it is out of their control, and it happens when great things are about to pass. It can be positive things or negative things that are to happen they just never know. But it is the constant "playing" of the **<u>Harmony of Light</u>** so that even as they relax the Darkness is on the run. This "song" keeps the Darkness at bay and keeps the battle being fought even when the actual being is relaxing. It is something the universe (God and Goddess) built into the ALBs and it is a useful tool, especially now. Michael tells me how magickal music and song is, how it touches the very core of the soul and how it can lift on to such heights never imagined. That songs of faith can be used to fight back when all else fails and how it balances things and keeps the Darkness away.

"So," I say, "are you talking about Gospel music"

Michael answers, "Gospel music works but it is any song that makes you feel good, any song that brings emotion to you in a positive way. These are the songs of faith and what you can use to beat the Darkness. Even your "Faith of the Heart" works cub, it makes you feel good right?"

"Yes it does," I say "It lifts you up, yes?" he asks. "Yes," I answer

He continues "It empowers you and you feel better and can fight back right? These types of songs and music tap into the core of the Creators, and helps to keep you armed against that which would do you wrong. It makes you remember you are love/Light filled. These are the songs of faith. My song of faith may not be the same as yours; it's a deeply personal thing. But the end result is the same you end up feeling better, feeling loved and feeling empowered by it all and no thing can hurt you as you regain the natural power you were given upon your creation."

"Wow," I say finally getting it completely, "that is so cool and it makes way sense. So this hum is the God and Goddess's way of making sure you all are empowered all the time and armed to do what needs to be done, even when you need a break. Michael the Universe is an amazing place and the Creator/Creatress are awesome."

He smiles at me and leans forward, ruffles my hair like one does a little kid who finally gets it after trying so hard. "That it is Cub and that They are. Now what do you say we split from here and run that race again, I won't take it easy on you this time or let you win?"

"YOU let ME win! Ha, that's a good one. Heck I'll even give you 5 lengths.

Everyone knows the South wind is much faster then the West. But if want to be embarrassed again who am I to stand in your way?" With that I jump up and take off down the hall, Michael just a bit behind. "You'll be sorry this time cub, I am so gonna beat you."

****

That's the end of that experience, I don't remember who won the second race but I suspect it was a sore loser who didn't want me to remember (hee hee.) The rest of it was interesting and I learned a lot, I hope maybe as I share it with you, you too will learn as I did a lot of information you didn't know or had not thought of before.

May we all grow in love and Light and may we forever work in the Lighted path and may you find your Song of Faith.

So mote it be
LWM

Personal Notes & Experiences

Energy Influx Recipe

For Frequency maintenance
    1 ½ cup Orange or tangerine juice
    ½ cup pineapple Juice
    splash to taste soda water

Jump Starter for toxic situations: To clear and remove these kinds of energies

    6 oz grapefruit juice

    dash salt

Personal Notes & Experiences

How to make negative entities run from your side, keeping anything within this circuit clear.

© Lady Wolfen Mists June, 2009

On one of my travels I spoke with Malik, who guards the Gates of Hell (see book Stop Kickin My Chair, story: June 2nd 2008 Meeting **Malik and the gates**) and he told me this little remedy. It's a powder that you can make and put it on yourself or spread around to make negative entities run from your side. These following items need to be gathered and mixed as explained. It may sound simple but he wanted to keep it easy so everyone could prepare it, yet powerful. Your main focus here is scent so essential oils are preferred but if you cant afford or find them a good smelling fragrance oils will work as well.

You will need:

1 clear quartz crystal (point is best)

1 Amethyst crystal (point is best but tumbled will work as well, degree of purple color isn't important

2 Rose Quartz (tumbled is fine)

½ cup of Bentonite Clay (get at any herb/health food store)

½ cup Corn Starch (get at any grocery store)

¼ cup sea salt (with sea vegetables in it if possible, get at any herb/health food store

20 drops of Lavender Essential Oil (This could be fragrance oil if that's all you can get or afford, get at any herb/health food store)

50 drops of Cucumber Essential Oil (This could be fragrance Oil, get at any herb/health food store)

10 drops of Vanilla Essential Oil (This could be fragrance oil as well, get at any herb/health food store)

Mix the sea salt in a non metal bowl and add the drops of oil in a clock wise manner (12;00 at the top away from you, 6:00 closest to you) Once all Lavender has been added mix thoroughly with the corn starch. Next mix the Cucumber EO (Essential Oil) clock wise as well, once all drops have been added mix thoroughly with the corn starch mixture. Do the same with the vanilla oil, mixing well. Allow this mixture to sit for about an hour to marry the scents together.

While this is going on place your stones in a non metal bowl, which you have physically cleansed and powered up by setting in the moonlight for at least 8 hours prior to using. Place them in the bowl in any arrangement.

Add the corn starch to the bowl. Mix with stones, so it covers the bottom of the bowl as best you can.

Next add the Bentonite Clay (if you cant get Bentonite clay any clay that is fine will do)mixing well in a clockwise manner. Now add the sea salt/oil mixture in a clockwise manner and mix all the ingredients as thoroughly as possible, blending and folding the items. As you blend and mix "see" the light from the universe centering on the stones and flowing through the mixture. The stones are setting the frequencies needed to protect and clear your area from negative energies and entities.

Once completed and all the energy you feel can be held by the mixture has been added let the mixture sit over night in the bowl with the stone, you can place in the moonlight if you like for extra zing but this is not necessary.

In the morning remove the stones and wash in running water. Put your stones away until you need them again. These stones need to be used **ONLY FOR THIS PURPOSE** and need to be stored when not in use.

Now mix your mixture once more and place your powder in bags. I like to use small muslin bags because they store well and are easy to carry. Store the bags in a dark place, we don't want the oils to break down in the sunlight and use as needed.

To Use:

Carry the bag on your person if you like, take a small amount, about 50-cent size, and rub on arms. Place some on each arm and on your legs. This sets up a circuit of light on, through and around your body forcing the dark entities to run from you and stop any oppression on your person.

To use in an area, just place a small amount in the corners of the room and allow the energies to set up the circuit needed there. It will connect the light and the frequencies needed to run the darkness away from the area. I would refresh this as I felt needed and at least once a month to keep at full power. You can place this mixture at the 4 corners of the houses foundation if you like and it will aid in keeping the correct levels of light and frequency to remove negative energies. I would refresh a house foundation, because of the amount of energy needed to keep the light anchored there at least once a week. I know that sounds like a lot but really to keep your place safe from negativity is it that much to ask to walk around and put a bit of mixture at each corner of the home?

Faded Scent:

If you have mixture left you didn't us but the scent is significantly faded, just mix the mixture in with the next batch your making and add an **additional** half of oils to refresh the scent. That would be an additional:

10 drops of Lavender Essential Oil
15 drops of Cucumber Essential Oil
5 drops of Vanilla Essential Oil

So that's it I hope you enjoy this new tool and I know you will find it as useful as I did. I carry some in my purse all the time and use it often on myself with I find myself in a situation I feel negative energies from.

Blessings
Lady Wolfen Mists

Personal Notes & Experiences

Celestite tool
For light flow like a faucet

© Lady Wolfen Mists June 28, 2009

In one of my journeys with Michael he introduced me to an Angel named Nitika. She was tall and lean and beautiful, Native American in features with long raven black hair and gentle brown eyes. She had a keen wit and a quick smile. Her wings were Nut Brown with Golden tips that left twinkles of light in a trail where they had been, very remarkable. Nitika is an Angel of Precious Stones and she shared a tool with me that we light workers can us just by carrying it with us.

She and Michael were talking about walking in the light and she had said there is a stone that you can use to actually leave a trail of light like her wings did. It would act like a ribbon of light that would pour from the person and anchor in all the area about he person. Just as the darkness would seek out the cracks about it and use those to break down the person, this stone would help find the cracks and fill them in, empowering the person with the light and heal the hurts. It would also help the user in spiritual development and help them in "learning" how to pray in a successful manner. Using this stone would help the person erect the walls needed to hold the darkness back and open the heart of those about it for the lighted path. The more it is used the quicker the time needed to focus the energies and the stronger the results.

The stone turned out to be Celestite. The crystal clusters seem best but tumbled work as well. The energies for all of this are already there in the stone's structure but you need to create programming to allow the stone to work like the faucet of light, making the ribbon of light where ever it goes.
Here's how to do that:

Items needed

1 Celestite cluster (size isn't important, something easy to carry is best)

1 white candle

1 orange candle

Matches and candle holders

Salt

Sit your candles in the candle-holders the white on the right of you, the orange on the left. Make a large unbroken ring of salt around the candles, big enough to sit the Celestite cluster in.

Light the white candle and the orange candle. Say the following as you hold the Celestite in front of you kinda between the two burning candles.

"Light of Positive path, from the center of the Universe I call you. Open the energies of this stone and flow through it."

Now pass the stone through the white candle flame 3 times, right to left, saying

"I dedicate this stone to the light and I pray for knowledge on how to pray successfully. I wish to help others and lift this earth to a higher spiritual plane, I anchor all my deeds to the positive lighted path and to the Lady and Lord of Light. "

Hold the stone now after you have passed it 3 times through the white candle flame, thinking on your higher self and helping others to reach their highest self and best clearest intent for all involved.

Now say the following as you pass the stone through the orange candle;

" This flame calls this light to this stone so it may flow constantly, in the highest level a constant open flow of positive lighted energy. That it may creep into all the cracks it finds and restore them to fullest working abilities, that it heals all wounds and hearts. Let this flow like a ribbon of light where ever I go and what ever I an doing, let this light flow all about me, anchoring the light to all and enforcing the positive wall of Loving energy to all who pass its way. Letting those in need be filled with its light and love and imploding the darkness that cant stand its lighted purity. "

Hold the Stone and see this happening, see where ever you walk there being a ribbon of light from you body, hands and feet trailing behind, beside and before you. See the light being anchored and cleansing all it touches.

Next pass the stone through both flames, 3 times (right to left) saying the following while passing it through the flames.

"Creators make me a tool for the light and lift my being to the frequencies I need to use this amazing stone. This tool I dedicate for all eternity to you on all levels of being as well as myself and my service. I have said it and I sever the light all the days of my life. It is done."

Once this is done put out the candles, clean up the salt and put away the items used. Place the cluster or stone in a special bag and carry it with you where ever you go. There is no repowering of this stone for it is programmed and will work in this way for all of eternity now. This programming can not be broken or destroyed because you have only released what is already there within the stone and did not place anything in it that wasn't there to begin with.

So that's another tool we can use, your arsenal should include this because it doesn't include fighting just carrying and would be wonderful for all Light Workers out there. If you don't want to carry it, then just place it around the home or where you work or even in the car, where ever it is it will generate the energies needed to do the job you have dedicated it to.

Blessings on your work,
Lady Wolfen Mists

Personal Notes & Experiences

3 Feather Prayer Protector

© Lady Wolfen Mists July, 2009

This tool was given to me in a dream I awoke and had to write it down. It purpose is to protect the prayers (or spells we cast) so they get to the universe and the universe hears them. Sometimes our prayers seem to get hung up in a web of gooey stickiness that the darkness weaves over the earth plane and are kept there. They do not get to where they need to go and the requests are not made. If we are not letting the Angels into our lives on a daily basis They cant step in and help, so this tool makes sure our request, energies spells and prayers make it to the ears of the creators.

Item Needed
Some type of polymer clay (for baking)

3 large feathers (Turkey feathers work)

Tooth picks

Paint (Gold color works)

Glue

This symbol needs to be placed on the base of the 3 feather Prayer Protector, it also tells you where to place the 3 feathers (as close to as possible.

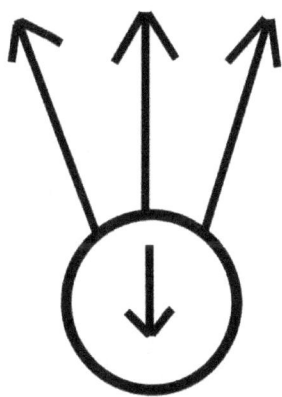

Step 1.

Roll out about a fifty cent ball of clay (I like sculpey but use what you like) Any color will do. I will use the color purple because it is for the higher self. Once you have a ball the size needed flatten it on both sides so it make a disk about ½ inch thick.

Step 2.

Take your feathers and poke a hole for each feather in aliment of the arrows above in the picture. Placing one in the center and then one on each side. You may want to place toothpicks in the holes to open them abit whit it cooks, turning the tooth picks now and again so they don't stick.

Step 3.

Bake the disk until it is almost done as instructed on the pack of clay you use. Let it cool slowly. Remove the toothpicks when you take it out of the oven , careful not to burn yourself.

Step 4.

When totally cool you can now paint the figure below on the disk. I like to use silver or gold paint as it shows purity and Light. Yet you can use whatever you like.

As you paint see the arrow/rays cutting through the gooey strings and webbing the darkness places about the earth and rising to the ethers tot he ears of those who need to hear. Then see the energies returning to you unobstructed, and answering what ever spells, requests, prayers you have sent Do all this as you paint this powerful symbol on your tool. Let paint dry completely before moving on.

Step 5.

Glue the feathers into the holes you created for them, let them overlap a little so they touch. Again as you add these feathers to your tool see the energies and prayers lifting without any obstacles to the ears of those they are intended for. See the darkness taking flight from your lighted words as you send your highest intent energies in requests, prayers or spells into the universe. See that the darkness holds no power over you and that your feathers cut through any thing they may have to hold you down. Now let dry completely for 24 hours.

Optional In step 4*

If you are good with the clay you can embed the symbol in your disk with another color clay and bake it into the disk all at the same time. Not being good with these kinda things I just paint it on. Do what works for you

After the tool has set for 24 hours we must empower it and dedicate its work. Here's what we will do.

You will need
A Sandalwood incense stick
A burner to place the incense in
Matches
A bowl of Dirt
Sprayer Water
A bit of ashes (you can get this from burned paper, just place in a bowl

You place the bowls in front of you towards the back of your work place. Place the incense in the center. Place your new tool on the right hand side of the incense, on the table.

Light the incense and let it waft up and its scent fill the room.
Pick up your tool and let the incense fill the feathers as you hold it over the smoke. Release the smoke you are holding by turning it sideways and say.

"I empower this tool to work for the light, like a lighted knife in the darkness it will illuminate and slice away all negativity. It will remove all bindings and it will release my words to the universe with great ease."

Let the feathers fill with smoke 3 times and release them each time Push the incense to the back now and pull out the bowl of dirt. Sprinkle a bit of dirt on the table and say

" By this sacred earth I dedicate this tool to the Light that it may for all eternity work within the lighted path. May it be grounded and powerful and may it help all who use it or who are mentioned by my words grow in love and light"

Lightly swipe the dirt away with the feather end of the tools; do this 3 times as well. Next bring forward the ashes, lightly rub your hands together with some in them and then rub them (lightly) on the tool feathers. Saying the following as you do this

"As the darkness tries to destroy I transmute it with this sacred ashes, I give it power to change and to transform that which would hinder and hurt to that which will

lift and help. So as much as the darkness sends to hurt and delay us this sacred element will empower and change it times 10. I dedicate this tool to the light and all that it does, nothing will stop it."

Then pull out the spray bottle of water and lightly mist the tool (lightly not dripping) as well as yourself. Saying the following

"It is by this sacred use of water I purify this tool as well as myself to work only in the highest interest of all involved. That my prayers requests, spells and thoughts be only for that which would lift this earth place closer to the light and further from the negativity of the darkness. Let it and myself only work to be able to become closer to the creators and the universe and that we may always work with in the lighted path.

Once al this is done once more bring the incense forward and once more fill the feathers with the smoke, only this time when you release the smoke aim it towards yourself. Do this 3 times saying the following.

"I am spirit, I am sacred and I am blessed. I am dedicated to the light, as are my works. I will fight as needed and I will win. My life belongs to the light and I work daily to walk my spiritual path and journey. I consecrate and empower this 3 Feathers Prayer Protector to the Lighted positive loving path. It is a toll against the darkness and it is anchored on many realms, it is unbreakable and will work to release my wants, needs, words, prayers, requests and spells to those in the universe for who they are meant for. This tool will keep the communication lines open and unbound for the return messages and ideas as I am meant to hear them. No longer will the darkness interfere with me and mine for I am the living power and I walk in the light, let it fear me for I will not turn from the light nor will my works. "

Once more fill the feathers with smoke and send the words out to the universe. Your empowerment and activation of this tool is done. Clean up and store you feather tool in a special place. Mine is on the wall in my room ready at a moment notice to work for me. All I need do is fill the feather with my words, intent and wishes and release them to the universe and KNOW they will get to where they need to go without any obstacles getting in their way.

Repowering is not necessary as long as the tool is used it will repower naturally. Nothing negativity can crack this tool as it is now based in the Lighted path an darkness can not stand the light long enough to crack it.

Walk in beauty
LWM

Personal Notes & Experiences

Align the Light Waters

© Lady Wolfen Mists July, 2009

This is a recipe I got from the Angel Raphael for those times you feel unsettled, down or out of sorts. It is for the bath or shower and pour 3 capfuls over your head as needed to clear and 'reset" the light within you. It helps to jump start your etheric healing as well in case you were in a battle and took heavy damage, which may happen in your sleep if you are a warrior for the light.

Items Needed
None Tap water
1-16 Oz bottle
2 tablespoons baking soda
2 teaspoons Salt (sea salt is best but any kind will do)
1 mixing bowl (not metal)
plastic or wooden spoon
nine garnet chips and sodalite (or lapis)
12 clove oil (fragrance or essential)
20 amber oil (fragrance or essential)
1   Cherry oil(fragrance or essential)
     *NO MORE then 1 drop

Mix the salt and baking soda in a bowl together, add 4 drops of Clove Oil, 8 drops of amber and 1-2 drop of cherry oil (what you like). Let the scent sit of a few hours to marry well.

Once the scent is set, pour mixture into 16 oz bottle (or split for 2 -8 oz bottles). Once this is done add the none tap water to the bottles and the garnet and sodalite chips . Close bottle and shake well, keep in refrigerator when not using. Shake each time before using. Do not keep for more then a month, throw away unused portions and make more.

Use with wisdom
LWM

Personal Notes & Experiences

Unbreakable Will Oil

By Lady Wolfen Mists ©1996

This is an old recipe I have had for a few years, it is for those days when we waiver a bit. When we are unsure and our will seems faulty and breakable. This strengthens us and props us up until we can gain sure footing again. It allows the angels to hold on to us and our spirit guides to help lift us, it calls other Light Workers to our side as we heal and repair the damage, be it emotional, spiritual or physical. It sends us a resound unbreakable will and allows us to share those energies with others in need. It keeps us tight in the light and we exhibit the unbreakable will of the Lighted path. When in doubt use this oil to lose the doubt and find the right way unshakable and unbreakable for you and your situation.

It is a wonderful oil and is used on the wrists and tops of the feet, as well as the crown chakra if you feel the need. This will make 16 drams of oil (or about 2 ounces.)

Items you will need
2 oz Grapeseed oil
Glass Mixing cup or beaker
Stir Stick
30 drops Amber (fragrance oil)
20 drops Nag Champa (fragrance oil)
2-4 drop Cinnamon oil (fragrance oil)

Mix the grapeseed oil in a beaker or glass mixing cup. Mix the Amber and Nag Champa first, then the cinnamon spice. Put in 2 drops and test to see if you like it. Put some on your wrist and rub it vigorously sniff, do you want more of a cinnamon spice scent then add the next drop or two. I like mine light but its up to you.

Once you have added all the cinnamon spice scent let it sit and marry for a few hours. Now pour the mixture into vials. I like 2 dram because they are easy to carry and use. But if you want to leave the oil in a larger bottles that's fine to. Just be sure to store all the oils, including your new mixture in a cool dark place away from the sunlight so the sun doesn't break down the oil.

Also be sure to label the oil so you remember what it is you made and date. These make nice quick gifts for people with a short card of explanation on what it is and how to use it; everyone could use a lift now and again.

Blessings and prosperity
LWM

Personal Notes & Experiences

Personal Notes & Experiences

Blue Kyanite Scalpel

By Lady Wolfen Mists ©2007

This tools purpose is to cut away any connected negativity that would keep us down or allow the darkness to feed on us, those ties that would bind us down to this material level obstructing our spiritual evolution to higher frequencies and levels.

Now Kyanite comes in small scalpel like shards usually and that's exactly what you need, just small pieces. Larger are fine and easier to handle or hold on to but for the qualities of the stone any size will do.

Here are the qualities of the stone as directed to be used in my tradition of Wolfen Wicca ® the ALBs agreed to these uses as they are the ones who instructed me to use this stone for the above said purpose.

KYANITE Blue (also known as Disthene)
Healing (said to aid on these levels):
This stone works mainly on the astral/etheric level. Yet it has been used to stimulate flow of energy on specific meridians, as well as cleansing chakra centers. It is also used to aid in the uncovering of "hidden" memories

Magickal & Etheric (said to aid on these levels):
This stone can be used as a scalpel (in blade like form) on the etheric/auraic field. It has been used to remove misaligned energies as well as psychic hooks. If you are going to be a healer this is one of the best tools you can get for psychic/auric surgery, however it should be used only by those who are maters at their craft. This stone is also used in past life recall, as it allows for clear memories to come forward. Aids in channeling and lucid dreaming.

There is no cleansing needed here or any dedication as the stone is automatically self cleansing and aligned to the positive lighted energies of the Universe. You just need to state your higher intent when using. Like this:

"I wish to remove any misaligned or connected negative energies that will obstruct my work for the lighted positive path. I ask for auric cleansing and healing on all levels, as I repair any damage the darkness has done to me (or name of other person you are helping here.) All this I do with the higher self-intent and for that which is in everyone's highest interest. "

Once this is said take a scalpel shard and begin (usually without touching the body) scraping the aura and etheric fields, as the stone begins to vibrate or become hot (or in some cases cold) know you have found an area that is being cleansed. You can also use this scalpel like a needle and mend any ripped or torn auric areas that may be psychically bleeding's. Once finished just blow on the scale, this blows out the negativity and replace in the leather pouch. It will do all the rest needed to cleanse and repower up.

STORAGE

You will need to worry about Storage; I think its best to make a small bag just to keep these fragile blades safe. I made a small envelope like bag from leather, for mine here's the lay out, be sure to add enough room for your hand to get in and out and not to snug. I also add a piece of cardboard to keep the bag stiff so as to not break my blades getting bent; it works well for me. The ALBs say to keep this in a Brown or Green Leather Bad if possible, this keeps the energies grounded and healing.

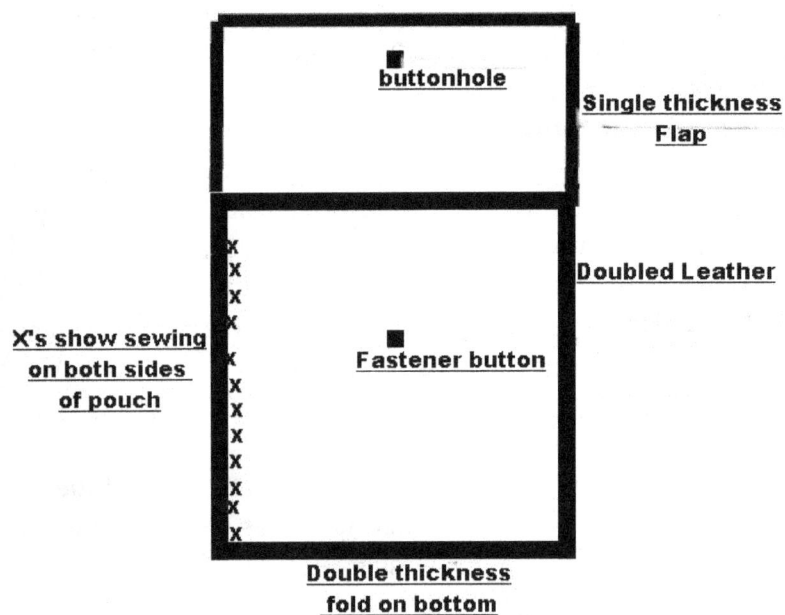

OK so that's it, easy to use and a must for anyone working for the light.

Blessings,
LWM

Personal Notes & Experiences

Light empowered Bracelet

© LWM 2009

This tool is to aid you in power control and in radiating pure Positive Loving Light to all those around you. By wearing this you light up the dark corners about you and allow others, as well as yourself, to see what is truly there and the potential of what could be.

It is easy to make and simple to use, as all you need do it put it on and it does what its supposed to.

Items Needed
Memory Wire (cut to your wrist size)
Needle nose pliers
Wire Cutters
Beads (6 mm is good size)
Sandalwood Incense & Burner
Matches

List of Types of beads needed
Rutilated Quartz
Black Obsidian
Rose Quartz
Lapis Lazuli
Ruby Zoisite
Garnet
Aventurine
Aqua Aura (Optional)

Before we begin lets state that I like to use 6mm beads but any size will do and some people may even want to use chips. I don't like chips cause they break easily but you can if you prefer. Now any number of beads is allowed just so long as you have at least 2 of each one mentioned in any arrangement you prefer.

Cleansing beads to use

Before we being the actual making of the bracelet we will need to cleanse the beads, to do this you simply need to place them in non tap water for about 15 minutes. Dry them off and place them in a bowl (with a paper towel in the bottom) then place in sunlight for at least an hour. They are now cleansed and ready to use.

Making the bracelet

Take you memory wire (careful it will scratch you on the ends) and wrap it around your arm so it goes around at least 2 full time, some people do more (I like more). Be sure to add extra room for the space the beads will take up if you want it to end in a specific place.

Now cut what you want with the wire cutters, careful not to hurt yourself. Place the extra wire and the cutters away now. Pick up the needle noose pliers and turn the end of the wire onto a circle or 9 figure. This is to keep the beads from falling off the end. This will be the end of your bracelet. Some people make the loop big enough to place a jump ring on and then place symbols on the ends later.

Once you have your loop you may begin adding your beads as you like, remember to have at least 2 of each beads, this creates balance and your tool needs to be balanced.

As you add the beads see them illuminating the darkness, see the darkness running from its light. See yourself being in control of the power the light generates and using it only for pure and truly good and loving purposes, see yourself gaining wisdom as your control of power grows.

Once you have added all the beads you want use the needle nose pliers to make a loop at the other end as well. This is also the time you can add the symbol if you like.

Dedicate the Tool to the Light

Now we need to dedicate this tool to the light, light the sandalwood incense and allow the smoke to flow over your new tool. As the smoke wafts over the tool say the following

"Great Creator(s) of the Universe Hear me, I have created this tool from the Angels to be in service to you the Lighted Positive path. May it work in the highest levels and may it help me and others. I ask that the darkness run from it as I show the light in all cricks and crevices and I burn for the Light. May my wisdom be great that I learnt o control the power this tool gives and keep me and the tool forever in the walk of the loving positive lighted path."

With that said pass the tool through the smoke 3 times right to left and then put it on, that's all there is two it.

Cleansing & Storage
To cleanse this tool just rinse in water, dry and sit in the sunlight for an hour or two. To store place in a special bag or box used just for this.

May your wisdom be great
LWM

Personal Notes & Experiences

Healing Glass; power of 3

© LWM 2009

This Glass is to be used with water to help in healing when one is feeling run down, spiritually depressed or out of sorts. Please note this is not to take the place of going to a doctor, it's just to aid in additional healing. So if you think you need a doctor or anyone of the medical profession please seek one out.

Again it is easy to create but you will need to get a few things.

Items needed
1 cup made of blue or green glass is best
Etching cream from a glass etching kit (get at any craft store)
Gloves for cream
Paintbrush you can use for cream
Crystal to activate and empower water
Water

You will need to cleanse the glass from any grease and then follow the directions of the glass etching cream. You will be drawing the symbol below. I have found it easier to make a stencil from contact paper and paint that rather then do it free hand, but to tell the truth I am a lousy artist! You do what works best for you.

Once you have painted the symbol on and allowed it to set, then washed it off you are done with that part and can put all that away. Next make sure it is good and clean as well as quartz crystal is clean.

Place the crystal in the glass and fill the cup with non tap water (is best but tap will do if its all you have). Place your hands around the glass and visualize positive light racing through the crystal from the center of the universe. See it flowing through the waters and empowering the monocles there with healing energies. See the life breath of the universe breezing into the crystal and then the water. Hold this and think on how it will illuminate your spirit and help begin the natural process of healing as these energy flow through you. Let the crystal sit in the water for 15 minutes as it fully activated the energies inside.

Pick up the glass and say

"In love and Light I drink this. Knowing all about me will energize and I will become whole, if this be in my highest interest I do this now."
Now drink a bit of the water, as much as you feel the need to, if there's any left just pour it out or feed it to your plants. Be sure not to drink the crystal!

Washing this tool is the same as washing any glass. Storage would be put away and used just for this purpose, Before you ask, water is the best liquid to use but others can be substituted if you like.

Repowering is not an issue as the glass repowers each time used. Be sure to use this crystal for this purpose only and keep it safe and clean!

May your Journey be filled with Love
LWM

Personal Notes & Experiences

Let Blessings Flow tube

© LWM 2009

The purpose of this tool is to bring the blessings you need and require to you. If you are feeling stuck and unable to move forward. If there just seems to be no where to go and you keep trying and trying but getting no where here's a helpful tool that may work for you.

The darkness may have boxed you in and you can't get out. Try using the 3 Feather Prayer protector in conjunction with this. It will cut the threads the darkness wove about you and this tool will call the blessings right to you.

Items you will need
1- 9 inch long clear plastic tube approx. 1 to 1 ¼ inches around
Silicone Caulking
Small stones (see stones list)
Chips (see chips list)

Small stones (at least 1 of each)
Red Jasper
Black Obsidian
Moonstone
Fluorite

Chips Needed
Garnet
Aventurine
Clear Quartz

To begin with caulk one end of the tube and let sit of 24 hours make a good plug because the stones will be flowing against this.

During this time be picking out the small stones you will need. They must be able to slide up and down the tube, small enough for the chips to get by but big enough to make some what of an obstacle for the chips. Cleanse these stones by washing them and placing them in the sunlight until ready to use.

Gather your chips you need at least one selection of each chip mentioned. Your chips can have holes in them so you can purchase necklaces or if you can find whole

chips that's great two. Make sure you have enough to fill the tube at least half way full. Cleanse these and place in sunlight as well.

Now 24 hours has passed and your plug should be solid, place the Garnet chips in the tube, now the Red Jasper and Black Obsidian, next the Aventurine chips and the Moonstone. Finally the Clear Quartz chips and the Fluorite with a mixture of the 3 types of chips to top it off. Make sure it isn't more then halfway up the tube, cause you will need room for the chips to flow up and down the tube.

Once you have the amount you want in the tube, caulk the other end of the tube as you did before. Let sit of 24 hours or until cured.

Now its time to give it a try. Think on the things holding you down see the stones taking in those obstacles and their qualities. See the stones becoming that which is holding you down. Now ask for blessing or specific request, like

"If it be in my highest interest release me from these bonds that hold me down. Like the tinkle of the chips that hammer away at the cords that bind me and let me fly to the Light."

Then turn the stick up side down and see the universe raining the answer you would like down over you like the chips that flow through the stick and around the tiny obstacles. Let them wash away the obstacles and clear the path for you or for another who you see that is in need.

That's all there is to it and its sooo easy to make and use, nothing about storage is special. In fact let it sit out and use it often. No repowering, it will do that when it is used, so go to it and make as many as you want. Everyone should have one of these they are efficient and simple to make

Blessings,
LWM

Personal Notes & Experiences

Chain Breaker

© LWM 2009

Here is a really simple and easy tool to make that will help you break the chains that confine you spiritually to this material world. It calls your Angels to your side as you pound and hammer away at the links that the darkness has used to bind you.

So on those days you feel down or depressed for no reason, when you are upset and not sure why this may help. Now I have to say if this goes on for an extended period of time then you may need to seek professional medical assistance and please do that if you feel the need.

This is incredible powerful when used with **Unbreakable Will Oil !**

Items needed
Key chain
Chain (at least 6 inches)
2 Jump rings (split is best as they don't open easily)
Sandalwood Incense
Matches and burner

Take the chain and place a Jump ring on each end of the chain link.

Next put the jump rings on the key chain so it kinds loops. You can get any type of key chain (usually at a craft store). I like the circular ones because they don't open as easily and the keys don't come off by mistake, but get whatever you like. Just slip both jump rings on the key chain, so it hangs down.

That's all there is to creating the physical tool, now we must dedicated it and activate it to the light for its purpose.

Take the sandalwood incense and light it, pass the tool through the smoke 9 times (in sets of 3) right to left, saying the following

"Oh Universe, with love that flows abundantly, hear your child this day. I have created a tool from the Angels that will help break the chains that bind me spiritually to this material world. I want to work for the Lighted Positive path. I wish to be lifted up and not allow the darkness to be in my presence or to hold me down. Each link in this chain symbolizes the obstacle limiting me that the darkness tries to use against me."

Now lift the tool in both hands towards the heavens and say

"Yet I hold the keys to breaking those chains. As I run my hands up and down these links I so break the bonds that they weave to keep me down. I empower my soul, my spirit, my mind and my body and I hold fast to the Positive Lighted path, for I am now and forever your loving servant."

Once more pass the tool through the smoke and see the bonds that are enfolding you ripping away. See them explode as you run your hands up and down the chain on the key chain. Feel your spirit being filled with Light and empowered by love, light and wisdom. Breathe deep these energies in as they flow through your mind, body and soul. Sense your angels at your side ready to lift you from this pain, sadness, confusion and hurting. Away from this place where you are bound and where obstacles keep you from moving forward.

Once this is done you have completed the construction of another tool. Carry it daily and use it often. Like I said earlier use this with the Unbreakable Will Oil and it is an amazing wall that works for you in a most positive way.

To cleanse and repower this tool just place in the moonlight (a window is fine) overnight and allow the moonlight to cleanse and repower as needed.

Great Blessings upon you
Lady Wolfen Mists

Personal Notes & Experiences

Random Acts Of Kindness

©by Lady Wolfen Mists Jan 11, 2005 11:13 am

Greetings Friends,

There is something that has been bothering me more than I can express, its how we treat others. I have been reading blogs on the net and I listen intently to the words, what is said and what isn't. I hear so many in pain. Some are in pain of normal life things, others are feeling shame over things they have no control over such as disabilities (physical, mental, emotional). In all cases these people almost always feel unheard and of less value. They live every day hurting and crying out and NO ONE hears them. They think no one cares, that they have been discarded and left alone awash a sea of shame, guilt, anxiety, broken hearts and most of all without any hope that things will get better.

My dear friends I ask you is this any way to live? Is this the way of the lighted path to allow others such loneliness? I'm not saying we need to "fix" it all, for karma may be doing something here and lessons are being learned. Yet we need not let them feel so alone, so helpless, so very worth less than even the trash outside. **So what can we do you ask?**

Well I do what I can, I share random acts of kindness. What does that entail? A coffee and sandwich for a homeless guy at a restaurant so he can get out of the cold. A flower (sometimes fake) on a windshield of someone who was hurried by 3 kids and very stressed. A smile and a hello to someone passing by (restoring dignity and respect) to someone who is often over looked. Its just that simple....something that makes someone feel good, feel connected, and gives hope of someone (often times anyone) caring.

I have even went so far as to make up small cards to carry in my wallet. They say: "***You have been Selected for a Random Act of Kindness! Why? Because you Deserve it!***"

I have included my two favorite Cards here for you to use if you like or you can make your own. You could make items as well to give away like candy or cookies or if your an artist lots of sketches. A poet could leave poems a seamstress could make small scent filled pillows or just about anything. Let people know you know they exist. Give them a smile. Make their journey easier on this planet and above all let it show in your heart you care.

I do all my work as **anonymous** because I love to watch the person look around to see who it may be that did this. I enjoy so much seeing a smile break across their face

and then sometimes even a tear. Its amazing to see the whole demeanor of a person change because I bought them a soda or gave them a gift of some type. It crosses all barriers of race, creed, religion and lets both of us feel that there is a greater purpose, a bond to all living things.

So please if you feel the same as I do, don't be afraid to reach out to that girl in the back office that has no friends, or the new guy on the job. Don't be slow to offer food to someone in need, if for no other reason than an endless pot of coffee and a slice of pie keeps them out of the -20 below wind and snow. They cant chase them out if they are eating and drinking (just give the money to the waitress and tell her to give the card to the person, you will be surprised at how the waitress is stunned at first and then watch the smile spread over her/his face as they become a part of the random act.) It is a scientific fact that kindness makes endorphins release and this is good for everyone. It helps in blood pressure and stress reduction and just basically makes you feel good. Give it a try you will make the world a better place and you will make yourself feel better as well.

After All the Mother and Father give us random acts of kindness every day, a rose to sniff, a bird to listen to, a life to live as we see fit…doesn't it make sense to walk in Their footsteps and do the same for others (as much as we can anyway?)

May you Always walk in Sunlight and Moonglow

Forever In The Loving Service Of Others
Lady Wolfen Mists

Personal Notes & Experiences

Greetings,
You have been selected for a Random Act of Kindness! Why? Because You Deserve It!

Blessings upon you,
Anonymous

Greetings,
You have been selected for a Random Act of Kindness! Why? Because You Deserve It!

Blessings upon you,
Anonymous

Greetings,
You have been selected for a Random Act of Kindness! Why? Because You Deserve It!

Blessings upon you,
Anonymous

Greetings,
You have been selected for a Random Act of Kindness! Why? Because You Deserve It!

Blessings upon you,
Anonymous

Greetings,
You have been selected for a Random Act of Kindness! Why? Because You Deserve It!

Blessings upon you,
Anonymous

Greetings,
You have been selected for a Random Act of Kindness! Why? Because You Deserve It!

Blessings upon you,
Anonymous

Greetings,
You have been selected for a Random Act of Kindness! Why? Because You Deserve It!

Blessings upon you,
Anonymous

Greetings,
You have been selected for a Random Act of Kindness! Why? Because You Deserve It!

Blessings upon you,
Anonymous

Greetings,
You have been selected for a Random Act of Kindness! Why? Because You Deserve It!

Blessings upon you,
Anonymous

Greetings,
You have been selected for a Random Act of Kindness! Why? Because You Deserve It!

Blessings upon you,
Anonymous

Greetings,
You have been selected for a Random Act of Kindness! Why? Because You Deserve It!

Blessings upon you,
Anonymous

Greetings,
You have been selected for a Random Act of Kindness! Why? Because You Deserve It!

Blessings upon you,
Anonymous

Greetings,
You have been selected for a Random Act of Kindness! Why? Because You Deserve It!

Blessings upon you,
Anonymous

Greetings,
You have been selected for a Random Act of Kindness! Why? Because You Deserve It!

Blessings upon you,
Anonymous

Greetings,
You have been selected for a Random Act of Kindness! Why? Because You Deserve It!

Blessings upon you,
Anonymous

Greetings,
You have been selected for a Random Act of Kindness! Why? Because You Deserve It!

Blessings upon you,
Anonymous

Personal Notes & Experiences

Seals, Symbols

In my work with the Angels they gave me specific Seals and Symbols for them and for specific situations. I share them with you here, the first one is Michael Seal, Call upon Michael when you need his help or intervention

Michael's Seal

NAME	MEANING	Tasks or Qualities	Colors- Stones
Michael	He who is like God	Removes blocks from dominating spiritual gifts. Chief duty: Protection and to escort any lower energies of fear away. If you are feeling warm in spiritual work it means this fiery warrior is there.	Royal purple Royal blue Can see colbolt blue sparkles in his colors

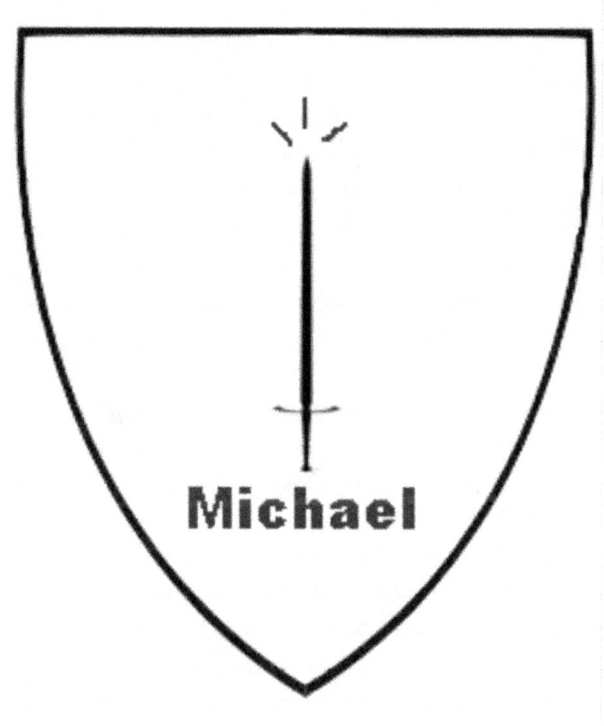

Raphael's Seal

NAME	MEANING	Tasks or Qualities	Colors- Stones
Raphael	Whom God Heals	Healing of people, spirit, mind, body	Emerald Green

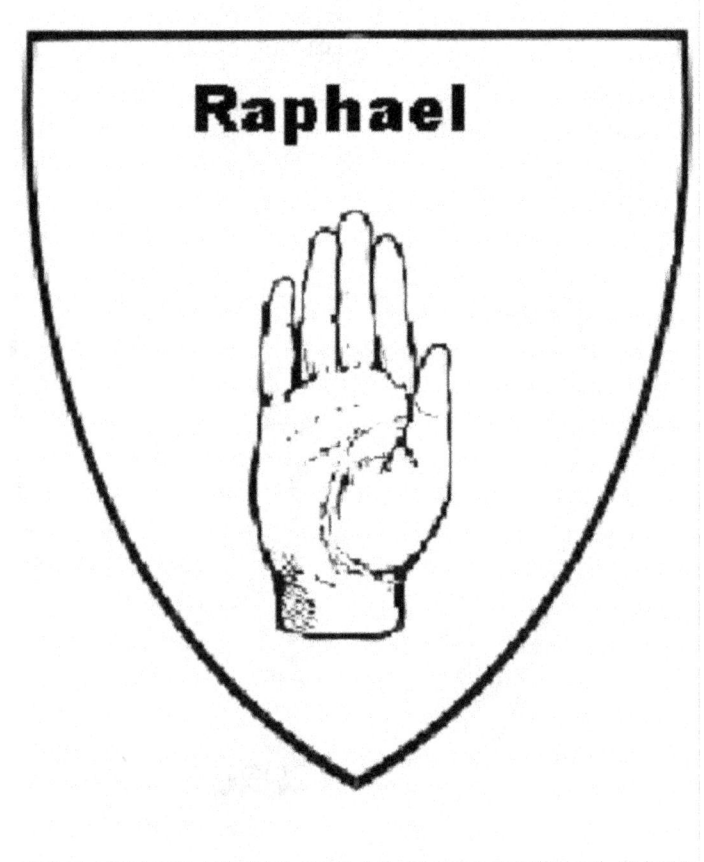

Gabriel's Seal

NAME	MEANING	Tasks or Qualities	Colors- Stones
Gabriel	This aspect means Gods strength	Annunciation's, Messenger Angel, Sends healing messages, helps you to tap into your strength; Creative writing, parenting, protects mothers & children	Copper, Citrine

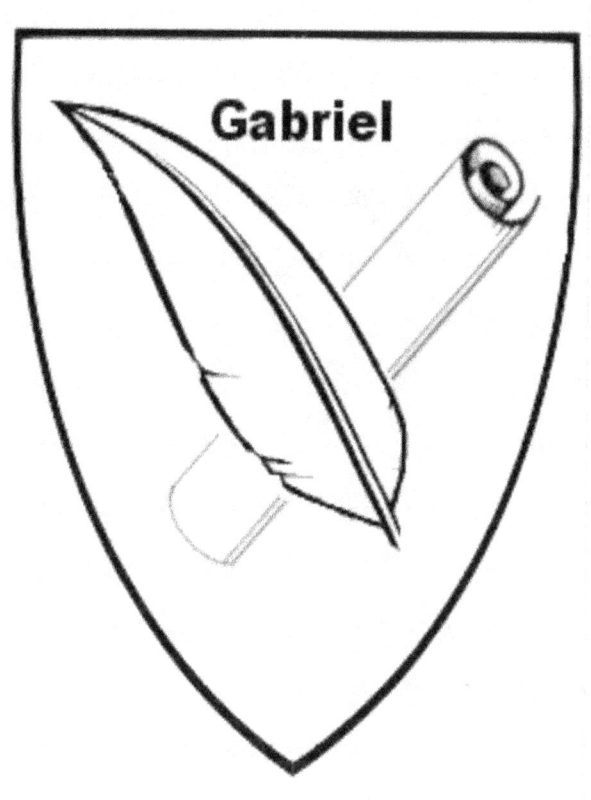

Uriel's Seal

NAME	MEANING	Tasks or Qualities	Colors- Stones
Uriel	This Aspect means "The Light Of God"	Angel of Creativity, insights into life, intuition, inventions, new business, teaching, delivers divine wisdom and inspiration. Illuminates cloudy situations. Only lights 1 step at a time but you will KNOW what the next step is to be!	Candles glow, Pale Yellow

Ariel's Seal

NAME	MEANING	Tasks or Qualities	Colors- Stones
Ariel: Sometimes said to be a fallen one but redeemed	Lion of God Lioness of God	Works close with Raphael heals Animals Bravery, courage, divine magick, master manifester highest will, attracts support for life s work/mission. Loves all beings especially birds, fish, animals near the water. Very close with environmental work. Supervises the realm of earthly angels that are sometimes referred to as the mythical creates we call fairies, elves, leprechauns, etc. These so-called mythical creates are very real beings of light known as the Earth Angels.	Pale pink

Isda's Nurture Seal

NAME	MEANING	Tasks or Qualities	Colors- Stones
Isda	Nurture Seal	Angel of Nourishment on all levels (physical, emotional and spiritual. Keeps all Pantries Full, on all levels.	Soft Violets, Soft Greens, Soft Pinks

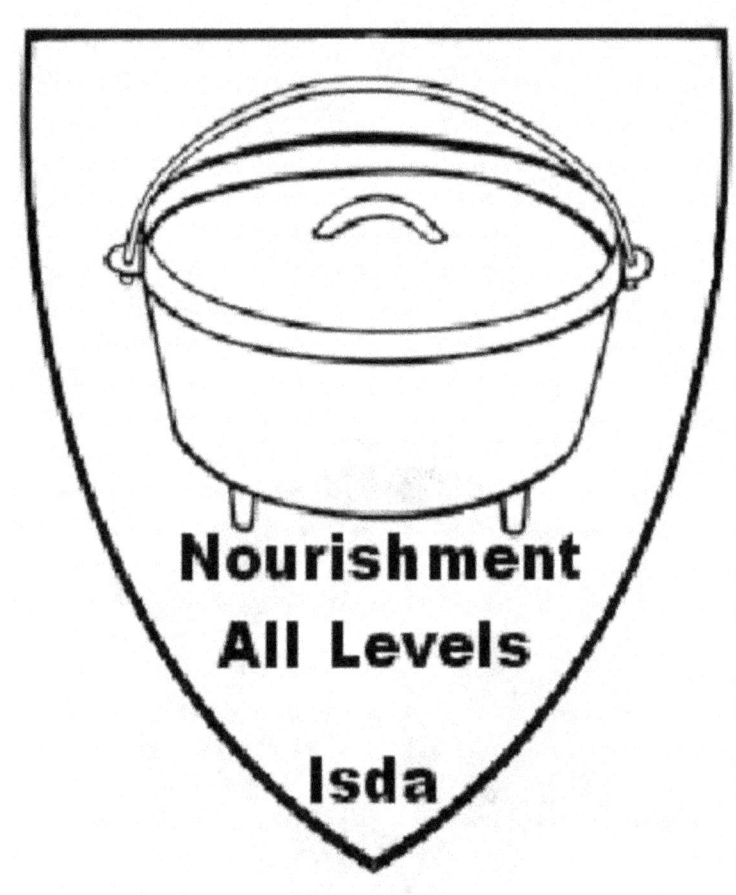

Risnuch's Seal

NAME	MEANING	Tasks or Qualities	Colors- Stones
Risnuch	Growth of Planted seeds Seal	The Angel of Agriculture, Harvest, crop success	Wheat Gold, Apple Green, Leaf Green, Pumpkin Orange

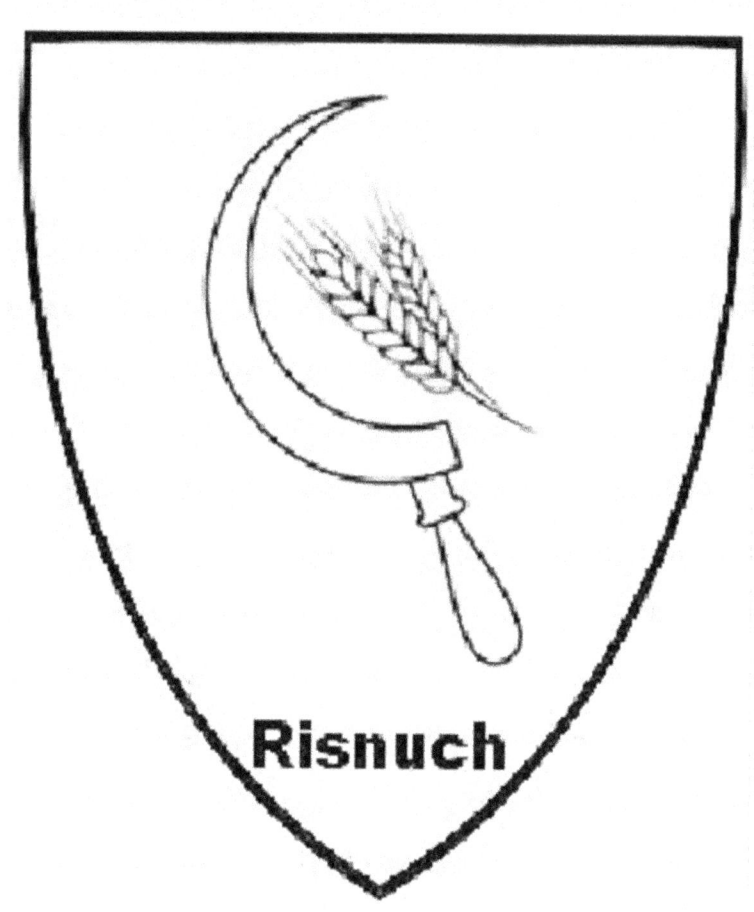

Personal Notes & Experiences

Symbol for Angelic Legion

© Lady Wolfen Mists Aug 8th 2005
All right reserved

    This is the symbol I was given in a dream/vision awareness. In the dream/vision I had been forced to take a chip into my body in order to eat, travel and live, I knew the chip and those in power were not of the light but I had no real choice. An Angel came to me and said to place this symbol on myself and I would be spared in any battles between the Light and dark and it would show (in a physical sense) where my heart was, on the lighted path. I put the symbol on me and in the ensuing battle I was not hurt in any way, while others were falling beside me. **<u>I helped with prayers and acts of kindness to all</u>** that I could as I did what I could to help the Light and anchor it to this planet. Ok so heres the symbol

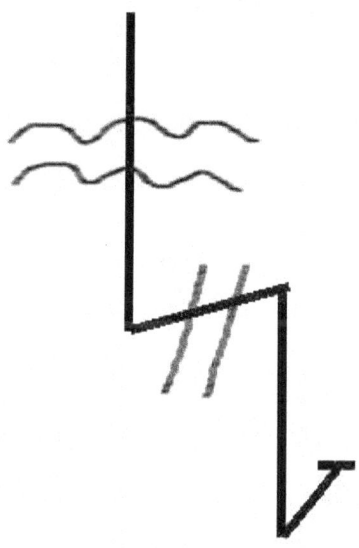

109

Use this to keep yourself safe and to identify yourself as a follower of the light, no matter what you may be forced to do. This symbol will signify you as a follower of

the Lighted path and a member of the Angelic Legion whose purpose it is to help anchor the light to this planet and dimension.

Please note that there are 3 waves on the wavy part and the slashes are slanted. You can draw this on yourself with ink or with oil or even the Dark Night Survivor Powder.

May you be Blessed in your work and may you stay forever within the Lighted Path
Forever In the Loving Service of Others,
Lady Wolfen Mists

About Symbols in General

      We will now move on to symbols, these are easy to use and very strong. In reproducing them size of the symbol does not matter, so you can reduce it and place it on a key ring or enlarge it to place it on a barn side. The only upkeep is to keep it clean so it can be seen and that's it. If you are placing this in the weather, you may want to "re-color" it now and again. The color you choose to make these in is 100% up to you, so look inside yourself and create. The only thing is they **MUST** be exactly as shown concerning what the symbol entails.

      Lets move on to our first Symbol.

Animal Protection Symbol

This Symbol was given to me to use in Protecting all animals. It can be worn on a shirt they may wear, coat or on a collar, tag. The other option is it can be painted, wood-burned on some material you can hang. Hanging on a door or wall outside the house will protect the creatures inside. Place on a barn door to keep barn animals safe. Posted in a garden or forested area will protect the animals in that garden/forested area. It aids in making a safe sanctuary for all animals, those domesticated and those not.

Protection of a Loved One

The Angels shared this symbol with me for the protection of a loved one. It can be worn, like on a back pack, even inside if you dont want everyone to see it. You can place it on a wall or door and it will protect those inside. To make it more person specific you can add the persons name you want to protect on the back. As it is shown here is will protect everyone in its range (approx. 3 acres in diameter) who you wish protected.

Reverse Negativity Symbol

This symbol is for those times in life that seems as if no matter what you do only bad things seem to be coming to you. You check everything in your life and use positive thought and actions and it just keeps coming, its almost like someone is sending negative energies to you. Well they very well may be, but you don't want to get caught up in their Karma so this symbol is what you need.

Manifest and Protection of Light Filled Beings

This symbol is to used by Light Filled beings who want to manifest things and have the ALBs protect that which was manifested. It can include, physical things like gardens or land to emotional items like shields to keep negativity away from someone who is being Bullied. It can include material goods like money needed or wealth to help an idea. Anyway you get the idea.

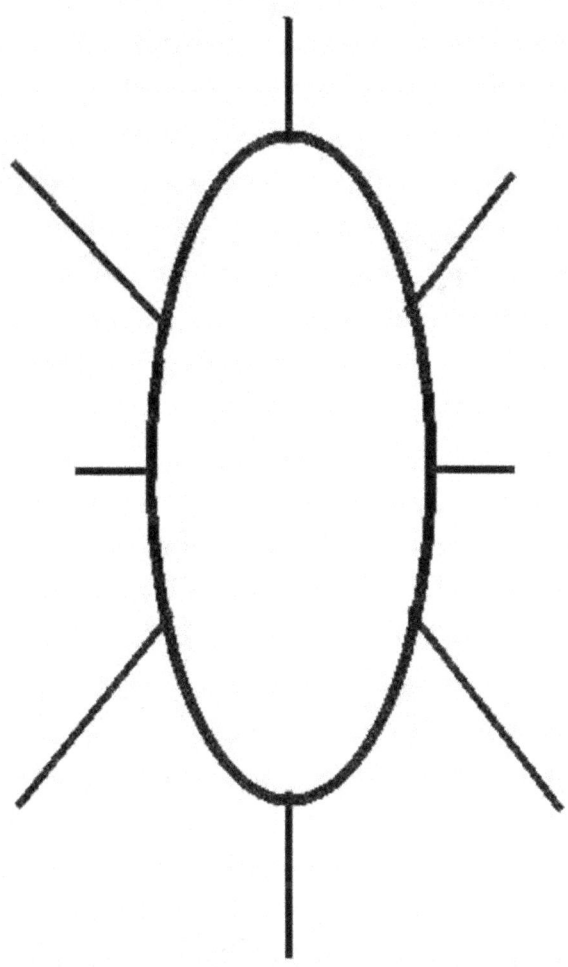

Manifestation and Protection of Light Filled Beings From the ALBs

(c) LWM 2007

Remove Negativity and Maintain a "clean positive house" recipe

© LWM 1990

I use this when I do ectoplasmatic (ghost or other negative energy) removals or House Cleansing's, which I have been doing with much success for over 30+ years, in case you, wondered.

Now depending on the spiritual advancement of the person who is being bothered and the amount of the infestation will determine how often you may need to reapply this cleaner. **Also start at the top of the house and work to the bottom,** because this traps the negativity into the earth and send it back to its dimension and doesn't allow it to flow out of the house back into the air. Once trapped into the ground you can use the Trapped Negativity symbol (see below) to keep your house cleansed. Any way here's the recipe:

1 quart of Distilled water
3 drops of Rose oil
3 to 6 drops of Sweet Orange Oil
A pinch of salt (not to much, just enough to dissolve in water, sea salt is best but table salt will do)
A pinch of Hyssop in the water (optional)
1/2 teaspoon of Glycerin (can get at any drug store)

Mix and shake. Place amount desired into sprayer, that is to be used for this purpose only, and spray around areas that the entity seems to be felt or seen around most often. Also spray doorways and wipe, with cotton ball, around any openings to outdoors (windows, exhaust fans, OVER (not on) electrical plugs out lets, doggie doors, furnaces (wipe on the outside of the furnace) and so one.) Do this at least once a week for the first 6 months, then as you feel the need, to maintain a "clean" house free of unwanted entities.

***Caution** Remember this is oil and could cause stains on carpets and cloth so be careful when spraying if you are worried about the possibility of stains) Any left over mixture can be stored in the 'fridge for about a week and a half, then you need to make a fresh batch.

With this recipe you can use the following Symbol for Trapping Negativity.

Symbol for Trapping Negativity

© LWM march 21, 2007

Here is a symbol I was given by the Angel Like Beings to help in the cleansing and Trapping of Negative energies. It is used to remove all inter dimensional negative (shadow people, ghosts, demons, and lots of other negative entities) beings as well as Aliens (yes I run a support group for alien abductees.) Before you use the sigil be sure to completely cleanse the house/area you want to permanently remove the negativity from and the add the sigil at the end.

Now for the Symbol the ALB's gave me this is the symbol that you will place (either in writing or in oil, in this case I like to do both just to hit all the levels of being). Once you have cleansed the area/house for the 1st time place the symbol at the lowest part of the area/house, it can be on a cement floor or a wall or such. You can also place a rug over it if you would rather not have to explain it to everyone. Please note: You will only need to do this once and it is done (any extra just re enforces the symbol.) Please do the horizontal rectangle first then lay the vertical rectangle over it next follows the circle and then the x (in no specific order for these lines).

Blessings, as we all fight for the Light
Lady Wolfen Mists

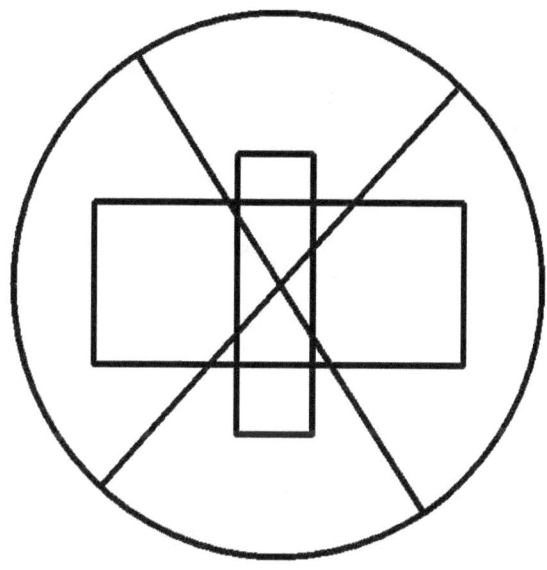

**Garden Of Angels Tools March 21st 2007
Symbol to Trap Negativity**

Positive Abundance, Wealth, Knowledge & More

This symbol Draws all forms of positive abundance to themselves. Wealth, treasures, knowledge, luck, happiness, security on all levels of existence. Contentment in Life. Protected by the very strongest energies.

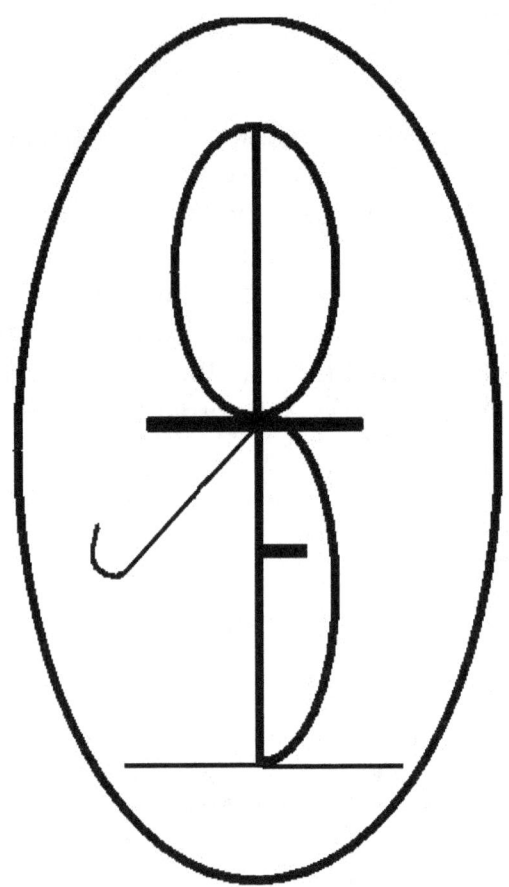

All I Touch Becomes Gold

Say this affirmation when using this Symbol. You can carry this symbol with you

"I am rich wealthy and protected. On all levels. My protection is unbreakable, All I touch becomes Gold. So Mote It Be."

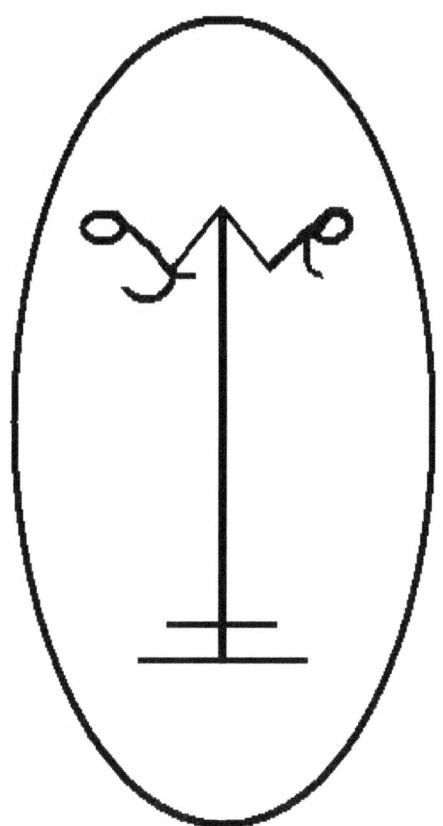

Personal Notes & Experiences

Personal Notes & Experiences

Personal Notes & Experiences

Oils, Sprays & Dusts

Unbreakable Will Oil

By Lady Wolfen Mists ©1996

This is an old recipe I have had for a few years, it is for those days when we waiver a bit. When we are unsure and our will seems faulty and breakable. This strengthens us and props us up until we can gain sure footing again. It allows the angels to hold on to us and our spirit guides to help lift us, it calls other Light Workers to our side as we heal and repair the damage, be it emotional, spiritual or physical. It sends us a resound unbreakable will and allows us to share those energies with others in need. It keeps us tight in the light and we exhibit the unbreakable will of the Lighted path. When in doubt use this oil to lose the doubt and find the right way unshakable and unbreakable for you and your situation.

It is a wonderful oil and is used on the wrists and tops of the feet, as well as the crown chakra if you feel the need. This will make 16 drams of oil (or about 2 ounces.)

Items you will need
2 oz Grapeseed oil
Glass Mixing cup or beaker
Stir Stick
30 drops Amber (fragrance oil)
20 drops Nag Champa (fragrance oil)
2-4 drop Cinnamon oil (fragrance oil)

Mix the grapeseed oil in a beaker or glass mixing cup. Mix the Amber and Nag Champa first, then the cinnamon spice. Put in 2 drops and test to see if you like it. Put some on your wrist and rub it vigorously sniff, do you want more of a cinnamon spice scent then add the next drop or two. I like mine light but its up to you.

Once you have added all the cinnamon spice scent let it sit and marry for a few hours. Now pour the mixture into vials. I like 2 dram because they are easy to carry and use. But if you want to leave the oil in a larger bottles that's fine to. Just be sure to store all the oils, including your new mixture in a cool dark place away from the sunlight so the sun doesn't break down the oil. Also be sure to label the oil so you remember what it is you made and date. These make nice quick gifts for people with a short card of explanation on what it is and how to use it; everyone could use a lift now and again.

***When Using Oils :Please use caution when using around cats, as cats can not always metabolize oils and can die from them. Please check to see if the oils used will hurt your cat

Blessings and prosperity
LWM

Essence of Light Oil

    This oil was given to me to help in restoring the Light in a place once the Darkness has been dismissed or ordered to leave. It is often used "after" a Blessing or Cleansing to help seal the positive energies and not allow the Darkness to creep back in. Usually the Blessing/ Cleansing works well but within 3 - 4 days the Darkness regroups and fights back, attacking with a vengeance that which it was driven out from. Using this daily, by anointing doors, windows and such keeps it sealed with positive energies. It can also be used much the same on people to keep any negative attachments from attaching to individuals. Lightly Anoint the forehead, wrists and feet if you like or just one place if you are in a hurry. It can be carried with you to renew its energy if needed

Essence of Light Oil

50 ML Grape seed Oil
15 drops of Myrrh Oil
10 Drops of Frankincense Oil
4 Drops of Rosemary Oil
10 Drops of Sandalwood Oil
2 Drops of Musk Oil

*6 drops of Dragons Blood Oil (Optional)

    Mix well, Store in dark colored bottle and in a cool dark place. Let it "marry" for 3-6 hours before using.

    ***<u>When Using Oils :Please use caution when using around cats, as cats can not always metabolize oils and can die from them, like Peppermint Oil. Please check to see if the oils used will hurt your cat</u>

Moon Willow Oil

This oil is to used to keep your self safe at night and open to the loving energies of the sacred night before a new dawning in your life. It aids in calling the Angels to your needs and wishes and keeping those needs/wishes in alignment with the Higher Self.

Moon Willow Oil
Grape seed base to 50 ml
25 Drops Cucumber Oil
8 drops Lilac Oil
7-9 drops Apple (or Apple spice) Oil
2 drops Balsam Fir Oil
1 Musk Oil

* 1 drop of Cajeput oil (optional makes it a bit sharper)

Mix well, Store in dark colored bottle and in a cool dark place. Let it "marry" for 3-6 hours before using.

***When Using Oils :Please use caution when using around cats, as cats can not always metabolize oils and can die from them like Peppermint Oil.. Please check to see if the oils used will hurt your cat

All Angel Anointing oil

Use this Oil when you want to generally Bless and Anoint a place, or Item or person with all inclusive Angelic energies. It doesnt ask for any special qualities other than a general protective Angelic presence and that Their Wings enfold you and keep you safe or keep a place safe with Angelic love and protection. An amazing daily oil, great in cars and in shoes as well as entry places in home or work.

All Angel Anointing oil

Grape seed base to 50 ml
20 drops of Oak Moss oil
8-10 drops of Vanilla oil
5-7 drop of lilac oil

Shake, place in moonlight, windows do well for this over night, then in a dark place for 3 more days to let the fragrances 'Merry'. Now you can use.

***When Using Oils :Please use caution when using around cats, as cats can not always metabolize oils and can die from them like Peppermint Oil. . Please check to see if the oils used will hurt your cat

Broken Wings Oil

Broken Wings (for aid in Healing the body in protection)

Another Oil from the Angel Like Beings. For those who are in need of physical repair. It is meant to help those who need healing, those who have lost their way. To help regain the physical power of those that have fallen or are beaten down in what seems beyond repair. Also for the protection of those we care for the small, the helpless, the hurting.

To Use:

Place a drop or two on body of person needing healing and rub gently. Allow scent to blend in and warm. As the scent warms more and more healing energies are released and are available for use. Ask aloud for the Angels to help heal the person physically. Use as often as you can or are allowed to by the person.

If using long distance rub

1-2 drops of oil on your hands and think of the person in need. See their situation clearly and see the energies surrounding them and blending with them once more ask the Angels aloud for their help. Do as often as you can.

Note:

If you wish to renew the energies and haven't any oil with you just rub the area where the oil was placed before (this re-warms and re stimulates the energies there already) and ask the Angels once more for help. Depending on how long the oil sticks to the skin it can be renewed this way several times before refreshing. You will know when to refresh by scent and how the energy feels.

For Protection of the Helpless, small and beaten down:

Place on person or clothing item or even favorite toy. Just make sure it is in the presence of the person you wish to protect. Next explain to the Angels why this person cant ask for aid themselves: for example they maybe too small, too broken to know how to ask right now (depressed, hurting, lost) or even a special needs person. Ask the Angels to watch over them and keep them as safe as possible. Ask that they aid in healing them as they may need. Request that the Angels walk with them so they do not become a victim of another who would do them even more harm.

***When Using Oils :Please use caution when using around cats, as cats can not always metabolize oils and can die from them like Peppermint Oil. Please check to see if the oils used will hurt your cat*

Broken Wings Oil

50 ML Grape Seed Oil
15drops Cinnamon Oil
26 Drops Sweet Orange Oil
5 drops Balsam Fir Oil
10 Drops Amber Oil

***When Using Oils :Please use caution when using around cats, as cats can not always metabolize oils and can die from them like Peppermint Oil . Please check to see if the oils used will hurt your cat*

Michael's Light 'em Up Spray

This spray was given to me by the Archangel Michael to help seek out and find negative entities that may be hiding in the dark corners and causing harm to all forms of living beings. These entities mean to do harm and eat away or feed on your soul. This spray helps Light them up and fills them with Light from the inside out. I ends the "Darkness" inside and the entities are returned to the Universe, their energy to be reused in a more positive way.

..

Michael's Light 'em Up Spray

-Need A 2 Oz bottle with spray top

-2 oz of distilled water
-1 teaspoon Glycerin to make the oils blend better with the water (get at any pharmacy)

With the water and Glycerin mix the following oils
- 15 drops of Cucumber Oil
-10 drops of Lavender
-10 drops of Vanilla Oil
-5 drops of Amber Oil

Pour the water, oil, glycerin mixture into the 2 oz spray bottle. Add 3-7 garnet chips into the bottle, to add the energies of the stone, and aid in shaking up the oils with the water before spraying it. Good for about 2 weeks in the refrigerator then you may need to make a new batch. Could be sooner if you see that something is "growing" in the mixture

Please Note: This contains Oils and may stain so test for color fastness and possible staining before spraying any area.

***When Using Oils :Please use caution when using around cats, as cats can not always metabolize oils and can die from them like Peppermint Oil. Please check to see if the oils used will hurt your cat**

Empath's Auto Shield Spray
Impenetrable

This spray was given to me by the Archangel Raphael to help Empath's Shield themselves from the many emotions they are often assaulted by. The darkness will often use these energies on an empath to drag them down and make the feel sad, lonely and hopeless. This spray helps to automatically shield from such energies and allow the empath to interact with those around them on a more even keel. If the empath wishes to lower the shields for some reason they can still do this, but they just need to rub the already applied spray, or re apply the spray to once more automatically shield again.

Please Note: This contains Oils and may stain so test for color fastness and possible staining before spraying any area. I like just spraying on myself after a shower and allowing it to sink in, then toweling off. Works well for me.

Empath's Auto Shield Spray (Impenetrable)

-Need A 2 Oz bottle with spray top

-2 oz of distilled water
-1 teaspoon Glycerin to make the oils blend better with
the water (get at any pharmacy)

With the water and Glycerin mix the following oils:
40 drops of Vanilla Oil
1 drop of Cherry Oil
2 drops of Peppermint Oil (can Substitute Musk Oil)

Pour the water, oil, glycerin mixture into the 2 oz spray bottle. Add 3-7 garnet chips into the bottle, to add the energies of the stone, and aid in shaking up the oils with the water before spraying it. Good for about 2 weeks in the refrigerator then you may need to make a new batch. Could be sooner if you see that something is "growing" in the mixture

Please Note: This contains Oils and may stain so test for color fastness and possible staining before spraying any area. **_*** When Using Oils :Please use caution when using around cats, as cats can not always metabolize oils and can die from them, like peppermint oil. Please check to see if the oils used will hurt your cat_**

Self Defense Dust

This recipe was shared with me by the angel Malik who waits, at what many call, the gates of Hell (for the full story please read my book *STOP KICIN' MY CHAIR*, by Lady Wolfen Mists section named **Meeting Malik and the gates**") He told me that this was wonderful for when one needs to act in self defense at any level. Large or small it is seldom known to fail and will not cause any negative karma, just returning and giving self defense to those who need it.

Self Defense Dust

2 Cups Chinchilla Dust (Gotten at any pet store)
1/4 Cup Bay Leaf cut and sifted
1/4 Cup Rosemary Bruised
1/4 Cup Vervain
1 Cup Sea Salt

Add the following oils to the blended mixture

30 drops of Frankincense Oil
20 drops of Myrrh Oil
20 Drops of Dragons Blood Oil

Next blend mixture well and let sit over night to "marry" the mixture. Place in cloth bag, cotton or linen work best, and use from bag. Just sprinkle outside your home (sidewalk, parking lot, grass) or place you go to often like a coffee shop, or where you may work for it to work for you.

Storage: Can be stored for a year or more, as long as bag is placed in a glass jar with a tight seal. Be sure to label jar with name and date created so you have a record. Placing on a dark cool place increase it longevity.

***When Using Oils :Please use caution when using around cats, as cats can not always metabolize oils and can die from them, like peppermint oil. Please check to see if the oils used will hurt your cat

Personal Notes & Experiences

Personal Notes & Experiences

Personal Notes & Experiences

Personal Notes & Experiences

Sacred Waters

Metaphysically Correct Holy Water

By Lady Wolfen Mists ©1982

This is a very easy recipe for Metaphysically Correct Holy Water. I use this in all House Blessings and in the removal of any negative energies, ghosts, or poltergeist:

1 quart of Distilled water
3 drops of Rose oil
3 to 6 drops of Sweet Orange Oil
A pinch of salt (not to much, just enough to dissolve in water, sea salt is best but table salt will do)
A pinch of Hyssop in the water (optional)
1/2 teaspoon of Glycerin (can get at any drug store)

Mix and shake. Place amount desired into Flask, that is to be used for this purpose only, and sprinkle around areas that the entity seems to be felt or seen around most often. Also sprinkle doorways and wipe, with cotton ball, around any openings to outdoors (windows, exhaust fans, OVER (not on) electrical plugs out lets, doggie doors, furnaces (wipe on the outside of the furnace) and so one.) Do this at least once **a** week, or as you feel the need, to maintain a "clean' house free of unwanted entities.

***<u>Caution</u>** remember this is oil and could cause stains on carpets and cloth so be careful when spraying if you are worried about the possibility of stains.) Any left over mixture can be stored in the 'fridge for about a week and 1/2 then you need to make a fresh batch.

I know this sounds really simple, I have been using it for many years, and it does work! I have had many satisfied customers using this simple but effective method! Let me know how it goes for you.

Blessings,
Lady Wolfen Mist

Blessings Water

This water was given to me for Blessing items, places and people in general. It brings positive energies to you or the items you wish to bless and focuses those energies in full, then seals the energies so nothing negative can exist around it. It simply negates negativity from its presence. In my experience it works really well.

Blessings Water

2 Ounce Distilled water
1 Tablespoon of Vodka
3 drops Orange oil
1 drop Amber oil
1 pinch Sea Salt
1-2 drops Glycerin

Blend together thoroughly and shake well before use, keep it well refrigerated when not using. Please remember this contains oil so be sure to test on items before spraying or anointing as it may cause oil stains.

Raphael's Spirit Scrubber Water

Use to cleanse and remove unwanted energies from spirit/psychic attacks. Aids in healing of astral body. Repairs rips and tears in aura/psychic bleeding. Renews "tired" spirits. Removes negative energies, renews and refreshes soul/etheric body.

2 to 2 1/2 Cup Water
2 drops of Lemon Oil
2 drops of Amber oil
2 to 3 drops of Glycerin
3 drops of Colloidal Silver

**1-2 drops light purple coloring Optional
1/2 cup Purple or White sand
1/2 teaspoon Lavender flowers
1 Malachite, Emerald or Bloodstone
1 Coffee Filter

Mix water, oils, glycerin, and Colloidal Silver. Shake well, mix optional coloring. Mix well. Place 1/4 cup charged sand in coffee filter. Pass liquid mixture through filter 2-3 times.

Now add lavender flowers to liquid pour into 2 or 4 oz bottle. Keeps approx 2 months. **Use 2-4 capful's to a full bath tub and soak yourself**

***Program sand before use:** Place sand in bowl (not plastic) add any of stones mentioned, Place inside a pyramid for 2 to 3 hours.

Raphael's Life's Green Fire

It is used to heal, settle and cleanse physical and spiritual sites (or items) from ingrained negative vibrations like rage, pain, torment or great hurt. It adds a healing covering over the affected area, promoting healing and keeping at bay negative energies that may seek to re enter the area (item).

Raphael's Life's Green Fire

2 oz water
7 drops Tangerine Oil
5 drops of Violet Oil
3 drops of Patchouli Oil
1 drop of Rosemary Oil
1 teaspoon Glycerin

*1 small Pinch of Rowan wood, saw dust size Optional

Mix all the oils and water and Glycerin together, then the pinch of Rowan wood saw dust size. Let sit of 2-3 hours and pour into 2 oz bottle, refrigerate. Use 2 to 4 capfuls of Life Green Fire to bath tub and soak yourself or items you are working with. If you can soak the items just lightly wipe it down with the mixture

Personal Notes & Experiences

Tea Lights

Tea lights

The Angels gave me this idea and recipes to share with everyone. It is a tool that you can easily create for specific purposes. Here is a super easy way to make your tea light please read it all the way through BEFORE you begin to create. There is nothing more enchanting than colorful, scented tealights, these scents reach out to the upper realms and call the Angels to you, the colors activate those energies both sent and received, so go and enjoy. Below you will find the following directions to create your own unique tea light candles.

Ingredients

4 ounces of soy wax chips or pillar candle wax
8 aluminum or plastic tealight cups
8 pre-tabbed tealight wicks
Fragrance oils
Candle wax colorant

Other tools

1 or 2 cup glass Pyrex measuring cup with pouring spout
Glass or wood stir stick
Sharp knife
Thermometer
Kitchen scale

Directions

Step 1.
Place the tealight cups on a level, flat working surface.

Step 2.
Place a pre-assembled wick in the bottom of each tealight cup. You will see a small indentation in the bottom of the tealight cup. The wick tab should fit nicely in this space. They may move when you pour the wax. Put a drop of hot glue at the bottom of the tab to secure it to the tealight cup.

Step 3.

Assemble ingredients. Using the knife, cut a small piece of the wax colorant about the size of a pea and set aside.

Step 4.

Measure 4 ounces of wax into glass measuring cup (with spout). Place in microwave oven and run for 30 second intervals, checking each time, and stirring wax as it melts.

Step 5.

Use thermometer and when the wax reaches 185 degrees, add the wax colorant. Stir for about 2 minutes or until well blended.

Step 6.

When wax cools to 140 degrees, add fragrance oil from your specific recipe and stir gently until blended.

Step 7

When the wax cools to 135 degrees, slowly pour into your prepared tealight cups. You want to make sure you don't have any air bubbles.

Step 8

You can adjust the wicks to insure they are straight while the wax is still liquid. Then allow the tealights to set and cure undisturbed for 12 hours or overnight.

You can make variations as you desire. You can add more or less colorant to achieve the color you prefer. Always remember to follow safe burning rules to avoid a fire hazard or injury.

If you find that the flame burns too high or gives off too much smoke, you can trim the wick slightly until you get the desired flame height. Tealights are very popular, and can be used any place a candle is used. It gives a room that warm inviting glow and scent to set any mood. Now you can easily make them yourself and enjoy them.

About Tea Lights

If the recipes below are to strong for your taste, "tweak" it as you like keeping the amounts equal in proportions to the original recipe

Bound to the Light Tea light

This tea Light is colored Electric Blue or Iridescent with Silver Glitter added to it. Once you have the colored amount of wax for your tea lights and the cups set out with the pre tab wicks added you are ready. The very last step before pouring is adding the oils need. You don't want them to boil too much because it breaks down the oils.

This scent and color ties the energies of the user to the Light. It states that they are "covered" by the Light of the Universe and that the Darkness can just move on. That you are protected by the Legion of Light Positive Loving Angels and that messengers of the Light are welcome at your home. You are a Light Worker and will aid others in that manner as best you can

Bound to the Light Tea light Recipe

51 ML of Carrier Oil (Grapeseed works well) *Approx 12 tea light

70 drops of Sandalwood Oil

20 drops of Cherry Oil

40 drops of Myrrh Oil

The Angelic Essence Tea Light

This tea Light is colored White with Frankincense Tears (or in place of the Frankincense tears sprinkle Purple glitter) through it. Once you have the colored amount of wax for your tea lights and the cups set out with the pre tab wicks added you are ready. The very last step before pouring is adding the oils need. You don't want them to boil too much because it breaks down the oils.

Use any time you wish to surround anyone, anything or any place with a "wall" of Angels. This aids the Angels in creating impenetrable boundaries through which negativity would be sent away, unless someone allows it to enter. It can aid Light Workers in becoming invisible to the strikes of negativity. It calls out to the Light and the Angels and says "Here sleeps a child of the Light. Rest here! Dwell with me and let us work together to anchor the Light to this world"

The Angelic Essence Tea Light

51 ML of Carrier Oil (Grapeseed works well) *Approx 12 tea light

65 drops of Nag Champa Oil

50 drops of Fernwood Oil

15 drops of Frangipani Oil

Sending out my Will to the Angels Tea Light
(Intersession & Prayer)

This candle is colored soft Violet or Bright Pink with Silver glitter added to it. Once you have the colored amount of wax for your tea lights and the cups set out with the pre tab wicks added you are ready. The very last step before pouring is adding the oils need. You don't want them to boil too much because it breaks down the oils.

Use any time you wish to send out your will to the universe to help others as well as yourself. Use for gaining spiritual gifts, physical healing or material wealth or such things as this. It awakens the universe to your wants and needs and focuses your request to the Angel in charge of that area. If it is in everyone's Higher good, success will be had, if it is not in the highest interest of all involved you will get a recognition of your request but the answer may not be what you asked for.

Sending out my Will to the Angels Tea Light
(Intersession & Prayer)

51 ML of Carrier Oil (Grapeseed works well) *Approx 12 tea light

80 drops of Oak moss Oil

35 drops of Lime Oil

35 drops Cucumber Oil

Personal Notes & Experiences

Personal Notes & Experiences

Affirmations & Chants/Prayers

Angelic Affirmation Fortune Cookies

This is an easy recipe to make Fortune Cookies. You can make them and place the affirmations I will give you in them and share with others if you like. I think doing it anonymous is fun, just placing one at a desk or such, or let people to pick from a bowl. You can also make a few for yourself or family and share them with them.

This takes about to to 12 minutes to lay everything out and prep the ingredients. Then approx another 5-8 minutes to cook, Remember each oven may differ slightly

Place a nice thin layer of dough for cookie on the sheet about 3-4 inches around for each cookie. Caution make only 3-4 cookies at a time on the sheet as they cook VERY fast and harden up quickly, so only a few at a time. This recipe makes about 10 cookies. READ ENTIRE RECIPE BEFORE USING, so you have everything you need

Ingredients to use

- 1/3 cup sugar
- 1/2 cup flour
- 1/4 teaspoon salt
- 1/2 teaspoon Vanilla extract
- 1/2 teaspoon Orange extract
- 2 large egg whites
- 4 tablespoons melted butter, cooled
- --- Affirmation strips cut up and made ready to add to 2 1/2 X 1/2 strips

Directions

1. Be sure to preheat your oven to 350 degrees Fahrenheit and grease your cookies sheet with a thin layer. Be sure to keep it well greased as you bake different batches on it. Alternatively you can use Baking Parchment Paper in place of greasing cookie sheet.

2. Place your egg whites in a bowl and whip them until they are light and foamy (on low setting if using a mixer)

3. Next pour and blend in the sugar, continue to whip this mixture until there are soft peaks forming

4. Now it is time to blend in the flour, salt, all extracts and melted cooled butter. mix everything until it is combined very well.

5. Take a small dolop of dough and place between 2 pieces of wax paper. Then using a rolling pin until flatten to about 3-4 inches in diameter on a prepared cookie sheet. Remember these cook quickly in baking and forming these cookies, so just a few at a time. You could also use a canning jar lid to cut out 3-4 inch rounds for cookies.

6. Still flat and thin (approx 3-4 inches) on the cookie sheet bake for about 5-8 minutes or until the edges are a light golden color.

7. Remove the cookies quickly with the spatula and place them on a flat work space

8. Place the written fortune strip in the lower middle of the cooked cookie still warm, then fold it in half touching top and bottom together.

9. Next quickly bend side edges toward each other. Seal the edges with a fork making pattern edges on the cookie and sealing the cookie.

10. Place in a mini muffin tin or such to help hold the shape until cool and crisp.

11. Repeat again with the remaining batter until you create as many as you like.

12. You can wrap these cookies in colored or clear cellophane and share.

Affirmations to lift you

I am open to receive all the blessings of the Universe

I will listen to my intuition and trust my inner self.

I am empathetic to those around me, but I keep healthy boundaries.

I am able to manifest prosperity for myself and others.

I am open to emotional/spiritual advancement.

I keep my temple/body cleared of all negativity.

I am proud of the unique creature I am.

I participate in loving acts and celebrate them, creating even more positiveness.

I acknowledge my special metaphysical gifts and accept it as a part of me.

I do not fear who I am, I accept all of me.

I have a faith/trust that the universe is unfolding as it was meant to.

I surround myself with kind, loving, compassionate people.

Even in my darkest day I react within my "Higher Self."

I call the angels to my side everyday so I may remain in the Light.

I practice unwavering faith in myself and the universe.

I am focused and clear in my intentions as I release my will to the universe.

I am not finished with life, all ancestors walk and are a part of me.

I practice kindness to all.

I love animals and make conscious effort to make their life better.

I try to be a light in the darkness for all.

I acknowledge the beauty in all those around me.

Whatever size I am BEAUTIFUL!

I "stand" tall and proud of who I am.

I practice humility.

I do my best to forgive those who I feel have harmed me.

I encourage those around me and share in their success.

My success is not measured by financial wealth but by the love I share.

I make time for things that make me smile.

I make sure those I love know that they are loved.

I am in charge of myself I give my power to no one.

I will nurture my dreams.

I will try to practice patience in all aspects of my life.

I will give my troubles and burdens to the universe and allow it to develop as the universe see's fit.

I will spend time with my inner child each month allowing it to play.

I will never forget how amazing and unique I am, there is only 1 of ME.

I will seek out my spiritual path and accept those gifts and directions given to me.

I will find my purpose in life all the while making it my true career.

I will do my best to live a health lifestyle, emotionally, physically, spiritually.

I will spend time wit nature to renew my spiritual energy.

I will try to think and act like a role model to those around me.

I will learn new ways and become open to trying new things.

I will become a mentor to those who ask.

I know I am not perfect and I will slip up sometimes, but I will try to remain in my Higher self.

I will try to do the right thing no matter what it costs me.

People are always MORE important than things!

I will learn to forgive and release the negatives that try to hold on me back.

I will do my best to SHINE!

I will show kindness to everyone.

I will do my best to give dignity to all beings.

I will uphold my word when I give it. A person is only as good as their word.

Chants/Prayers

This chant was given to me to say when I needed an extra boost to feel safe.

Hear me now,
Make it so!
Keep me safe wherever I go!

****

This chant is to make it clear to any that may doubt where this Spirit Warrior stands

In the Night I do see
Positive energies flowing over me

In the Day I can feel their touch
Angles speak and say so much

I am a Servant of the Light
To this side I bind my fight

****

For those who seek a restful sleep. Maybe you are attacked when sleeping, or have nightmares. Maybe you wish to speak to the Creators in your dream time and do not wish to be blocked by lower level entities. This little Prayer Chant will help;

Universe protect me as I sleep
Safely at the Creators Feet
May the Angels secure and strong
Hold me close all night long

As I sleep within their Wings
Feathers soft and I'm unseen
Darkness passes me by
While in restful sleep I lie

****

For those hurting from gossip, lies, oppression and just painful acts of those who would do you harm

This path is painful that I walk
Blind, Alone with no one to talk
Oppressors surround me all about
I am broken, to torn to shout out

Yet as I cry I feel your touch
I hear your feathers and I am lifted up
My Guardian swoops in and carries me
Up to the healing light so I can see

I am healed and I am wholly me

****

For someone wishing gifts from the universe based in Loving Positive energies

Universe I call to me
Wisdom, wealth and prosperity
Shield me from my oppressors, and negativity
Grounded In the Light, like a grand Oak tree
All this dear Universe I call to me.

****

For one who wishes there to be no doubt they are a child of the Loving Positive Light and will always be so. For those times when you may be frightened and need to put on a bit more "armor."

I am lifted by the Light.
No darkness here within my sight.
I serve the Light with all my heart
Darkness hear me, NOW depart

****

For one who has crossed over but you want to honor and keep safe

**Hail the traveler who walks on without fear
You will be missed each day here
In my heart I will keep our memories there
May your passing be clean and without care
Until we meet again, my friend I say
"Come retrieve me on my crossing day."**

Personal Notes & Experiences

Personal Notes & Experiences

Fabric Tools

How to use these items

These fabric items are patterns and symbols that you can use for specific purposes. They can be embroidered on fabric, craft painted, needlepoint or anything like this. Many can be placed on pillows or clothing pieces or even blankets. Your imagination sets the limits. Anything that is SPECIFIC to that symbol or tool will be noted at the top of each item.

Be sure to place these items out in the "viewing" area of people (IE the couch, or throw for back of couch). This allows the energies contained and stimulated by the tool to be "working" and doing for you what it is "programmed" to do. If you give these as gifts just make sure the person it is meant for (or a family member if it is for a family) touches it. This releases your energies and intent as well as the energies of the actual tool itself for those it was created for.

Enjoy and allow the Angels to be a part of your daily environment!

To Banish Demons and Negativity

This tool was given to me by the Angels to aid in getting rid of any negative entities or Demons that may be following or oppressing you. It can be done 1 of 2 ways.

1. Inside the book as shown (figure A)
2. The symbol alone (figure B)

Figure A

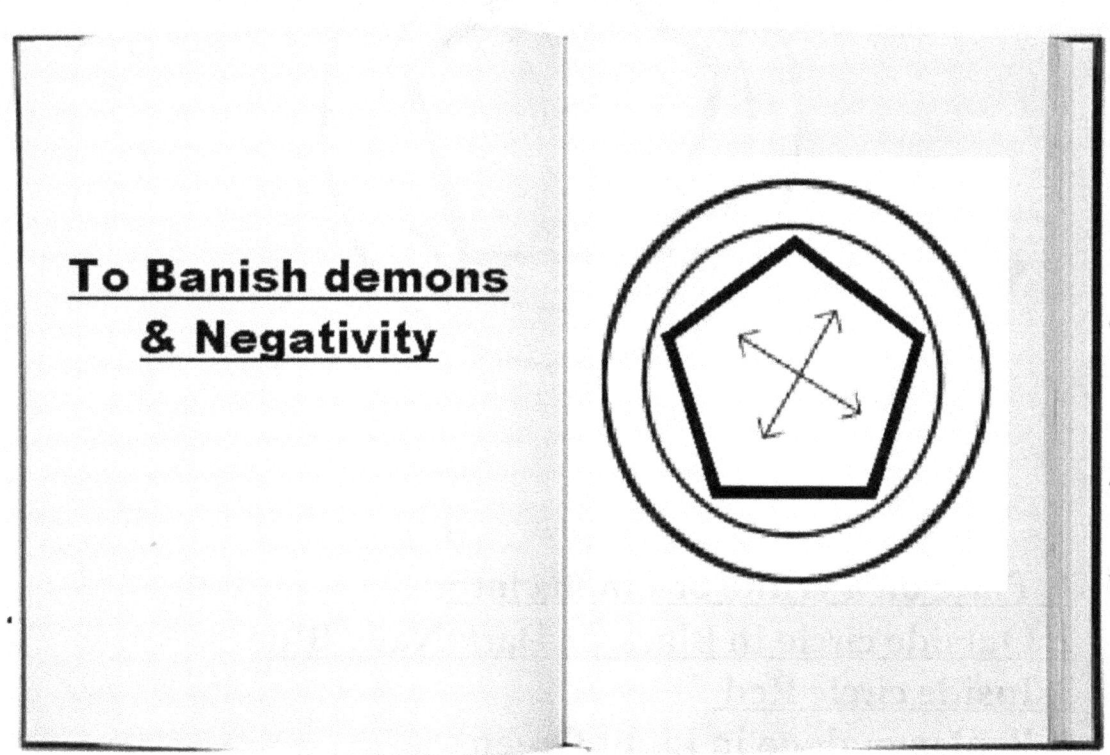

1. **Words in black**
2. **Outside circle in Black or Dark Navy Blue**
3. **Inside circle Red**
4. **Pentagon done in Light Green**

<u>**5. Arrows in Bright Yellow**</u>
<u>**6. Book edges in Brown or Tan**</u>

<u>Figure B</u>

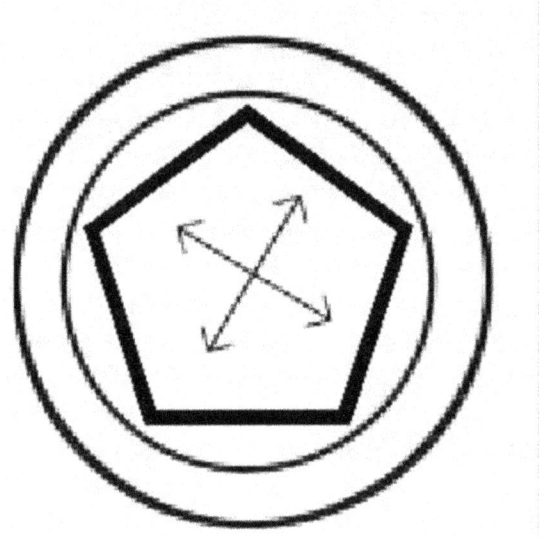

<u>*1.* **Place on a White or Linen cloth**</u>
<u>**2. Outside circle in Black or Dark Navy Blue**</u>
<u>**3. Inside circle Red**</u>
<u>**4. Pentagon done in Light Green**</u>
<u>**5. Arrows in Bright Yellow**</u>

Blessing of a New Life or Home

This Angelic tool is used to bless a home or someones new life. It can be used when you move to a new place to live or a new job space or dorm. In addition to that it can be used when one begins a new life, like starting over after a divorce or going to college, or just trying over again.

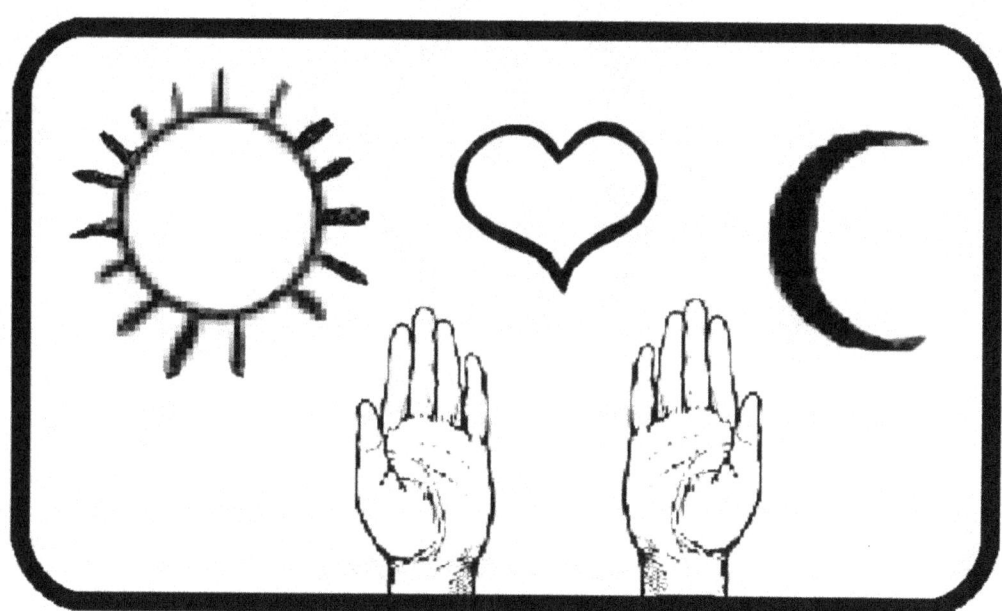

1. Frame is Purple
2. Sun is Orange and Yellow
3. Heart is Red or Pink
4. Moon is Silver or Gray
5. Hands are Flesh
   (the color of the skin of the person this is being created for)

Protection from all forms of Extreme Weather

This tool was given to me from the Angels in reference to all the unusual weather that has been occurring around the world. So if you are living in an area prone to such extremes you may wish to us this. It can also be added to a backpack to aid children / students as well.

1. Triangle is Green
2. Outside Line Star is Light Blue
3. Inside Line Star is Bright Purple

Bring Wealth & Gifts to someone
Material, Spiritual, Mentally

This tool is used to aid a person in being Blessed with all forms of Wealth and Gifts. These gifts and wealth can be on physical, emotional and spiritual levels.

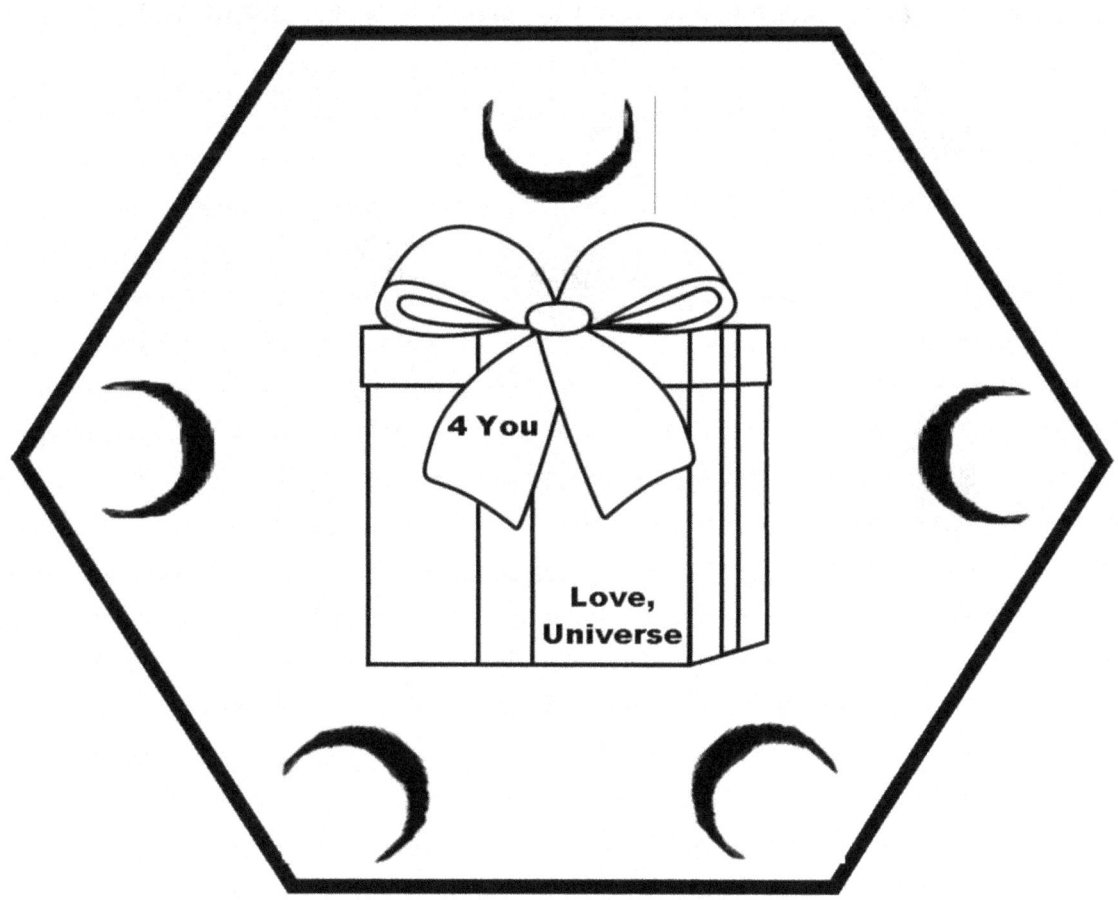

1. Outside is Purple
2. Moons Very Top Silver, Top Right is Green. Right Bottom is Yellow, Bottom left is Red, Top Left is Blue
3. Ribbon lines is Red
4. Words are Black

Surrounded By the Light

This Angels tool was given to me on a bad day when oppression and depression was overwhelming me. This tool is to aid such things and lets the user sleep in comfort knowing they are surrounded by the Light. I like the idea that these can be used in the bedroom (pillowcase or blanket) letting the sleeper know they are surrounded by the Light while sleeping. It can also be used when going out in public like on a key chain or patch inside a coat or on a back pack. Your ideas are limitless.

Please Note that the banner in the center of the symbol can have a specific single first name or the entire family name.

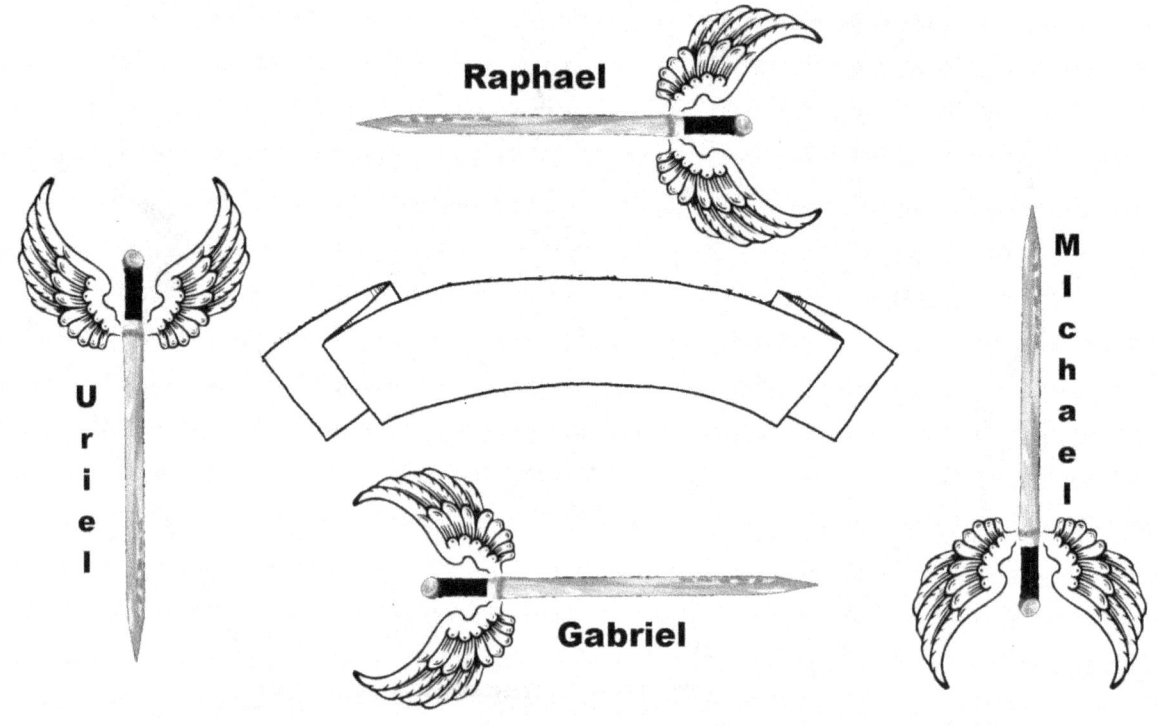

1. **All Wings are out lined in Light Blue (Robin Egg)**
2. **All Sword Handles are Black**
3. **The Raphael Sword Blade is to be in Emerald Green**

4. The Michael Sword Blade is to be in Royal Blue or Royal Purple

5. The Sword Blade Gabriel is Copper Citrine (yellow with flecks of copper or brown)
6. The sword Blade of Uriel is soft candles glow Yellow, can have flecks of Orange
7. The Banner Outline is Red
8. The name is done in Black (it can be for a single person by using the first name, or for an entire family by using the last name)

Legion Of Light Pillow

This is of course my old stand by, I use this symbol daily and now here it is as a throw pillow for the entire family home environment. The Angels suggested that this be on a throw pillow form and for it to be given away as gifts. It assures that this family are servants of the Light, the Positive Loving Light and only positive energies are welcome. It tells the Angels they are welcome their as well.

Color Instructions
1. The circle is Bright Aqua Blue
2. The entire Frame is Black
3. The 2 Waves are Blue/green (Teal)
4. The 2 Slashes through the frame are Bright Yellow

Sorry, this template is so big it needed a whole page to itself, see figure.

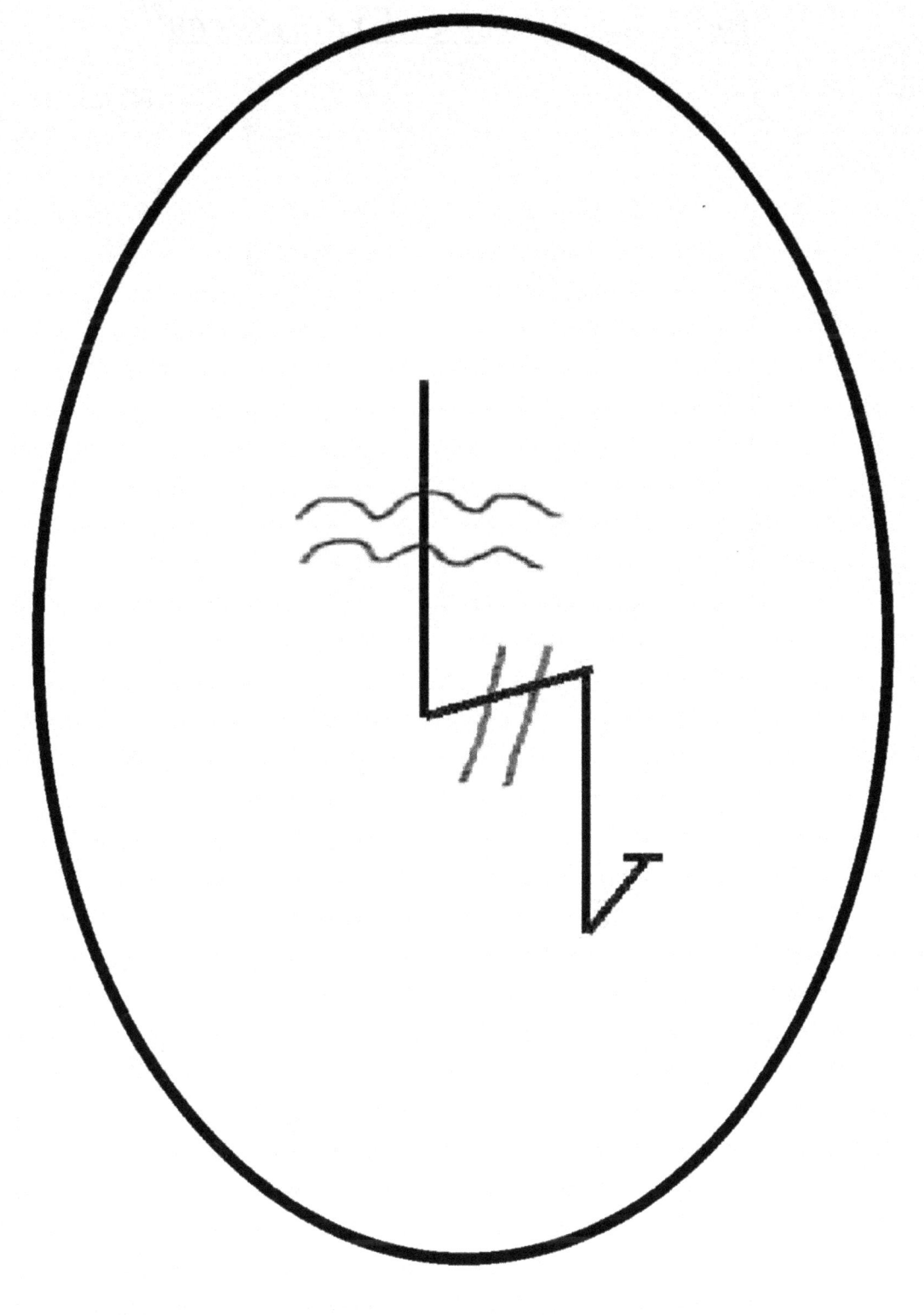

Personal Notes & Experiences

Personal Notes & Experiences

Personal Notes & Experiences

Tools That Don't Fit Anywhere Else

DARKNESS vs dark/shadow self; What they are

copyright by Lady Wolfen Mists 11/25/2014

Alright no more putting it off, here is what the Angels have been pushing me to write. The Difference between the DARKNESS and the dark/shadow self. I haven't wanted to write it cause I know its gonna open a can of worms and I am not really up to the arguments, but one can not fight the Angels, they always win with me. So angels let your energies flow and lets get started.

Lets start with the shadow self and what that is by my definition. It is the dark half of the self we all have, the Negative polarity wise, that we are all born with. It is a part of you and **must** be honored, just as the Light half or Positive half is honored. One should never strive to remove the dark half of the self for that would put the soul out of sync and not be true to who you are. Sure the dark half is there and we all sometimes have dark, sad hurtful thoughts. But we **Choose** not to dwell in them and to keep ourselves balanced. Without the dark half we would not feel pain at the crossing of a loved one, or cry when we hurt.

There is a balance that is struck within us between the positive and negative polarities and we work to keep that balance. I have never promoted that one should totally remove the dark/shadow self but one should work within the light and keep all things balanced. The dark/shadow self has its place and is kept there, it does not war with the light and lives side by side when both are in tune. If either side positive or negative is related to too much and allowed to control the self then that also is bad for the self. **All things in moderation** and that includes both the polarities we are all born with. Acknowledge within the dark/shadow self and let your actions be those that helps keep you on the lighted path. Just because you acknowledge the dark part of the self and honor it does not mean you have to choose to live there in the dark half.

Now on to the DARKNESS. The DARKNESS is an entity/energy in the universe that is not content to lay side by side with the LIGHT. It wants to control and feed off the LIGHT, wants to destroy all LIGHT and has no room for anything else. The DARKNESS is not willing to compromise, it's one ultimate task is to bring hurt and pain to all. The DARKNESS finds joy, happiness and bliss in keeping so many from their spiritual path and away from a spiritual connection to the Creator(s). The DARKNESS is always in a battle with the LIGHT and will attack anyone or anything that works for the LIGHT. The DARKNESS feeds off of us, off our fear, anger, hurt, depression, drug use and anything else that might tie us down to the lower levels of being. One can not reason with the DARKNESS for it is centered on harming all and feeding off of them, controlling their every action. Once done it moves on to the next. All that can be done is to Battle the DARKNESS and send it back to the Universe so that its energy can be reused in a more positive manner that would help everyone.

Have you never noticed that often when you do something good for another that something bad comes seeking you? That is the DARKNESS keeping you from doing more Lighted positive things, Do these things anyway for it lifts your very soul and those you help. The DARKNESS can not have this so it puts obstacles and painful things in your way to get you to refocus your energy. To keep you from helping others and to think only of your problems. When this happens STOP! Take a deep breath and say;

"DARKNESS I know you are there. I will not serve you, I will not fear you. I will fight again and again no matter how many times I fall, for I am a servant of the Lighted Loving Positive path"

The battle to keep the DARKNESS from taking your soul (feeding off of it and confining you to these lower realms of being) is on going, and if you are a Light Warrior or a Light Worker, you know what I am trying to say. We must not let this Darkness win or we (all beings who live in this realm) are doomed to remain separated from the Higher more spiritual realms and serving the DARKNESS as it feeds off our very life essence.

Ok you say, I get that, but what can I a single person do? Do good things, reach out when you can, show compassion, sing, be joyful, be grateful, lift others up, find your spiritual center and work from there, practice acceptance of others, and above all LOVE. That my friends will not just remove the DARKNESS (and send it to be reused in a more positive way by the universe) It will also lift this whole plane of existence up to higher levels, bringing us closer to the Creator(s) and to our true Higher Self's.

Well now that is done and it wasn't as hard as I thought it would be. There is much more in depth but for many of you I hope this will be enough to get the point across. No one is asking you to deny your shadow/dark self or not to be all of who you are. No! We are asking you to join in with this battle against the DARKNESS and help lift this world/plane to a higher level. To be balanced in your actions/work and LOVE, that is all.

Anti-Vampire Sachet

All of us know that person that comes along and just seems to never give out any positive energy. In fact you find yourself tired and exhausted in their presence. Sometimes it seems to go so far as to make one feel physically ill. The Angels gave me these tiny sachets to carry or place above your doors to keep these psychic energy vamps away from you. They are great to place over you bedroom doorway to keep these vampires away from you as you sleep. You can take them to work and place over entrance's there or on your desk. Students can place them in lockers or backpaks. Let you intuition guide you.

Anti-Vampire Sachet

15 drops of Cypress Oil
10 drops of Bay Laurel Oil
21 drops of Lilly of the Valley oil

1/2 cup Mint Leaves
1 cup of Oat Moss
!/4 Cup Poppy seed
1/4 cup of Rosemary (broken and bruised)

***When Using Oils :Please use caution when using around cats, as cats can not always metabolize oils and can die from them, like Peppermint Oil. Please check to see if the oils used will hurt your cat**

Sacred Ground Resins

These resins help to create Sacred Ground energies where ever it is sitting out. i can be burned on an incense charcoal Burner or just left to sit out. The Angels speak how this is a quick way to create sacred ground and keep negative energies and spirits out of the area.

Sacred Ground Resins

1/2 cup of Myrrh Resin
1/2 cup of Copal Resin
1/2 Cup of Frankincense Resin
1/2 cup of Sandalwood Powder or Chips
1/4 cup of Dragons Blood Resin

Angel World Terrarium

Make a small Terrarium which would be great for where you work, add plants you like except cactus. Then add decorative stones for whatever particular angel you wish to surround yourself with. You will feel the guidance and qualities of this Angel within days of the creation of this Tool.

If you wish to have more than one Angel symbolized in your Terrarium then make it bigger and add that angels stones as well. No need to worry about offending anyone as they all work well together. You can also add Angel like decorations in you Terrarium as well.

Its yours so make it magickal and meditate to the Angel when you need to "speak" with them or you need to access their helpful qualities. Here is a list of the 7 Archangels as I see and Know them to get you started .

Name	Meanings	Stones
Michael	He who is like God	Sugalite. Chevron Amethyst
Raphael	Whom God Heals	Malachite, Emerald
Chamuel	He who sees God	Green fluorite Green calcite
Uriel	This Aspect means "The Light Of God"	Amber
Zadkiel	This aspect means Mercy of God	Lapis Lazuli
Gabriel	This aspect means Gods strength	Copper or Citrine
Haniel	This aspect means Glory of God	Moonstone

Personal Notes & Experiences

Personal Notes & Experiences

All Acts of Light for a Year

ACTS OF LIGHT

These are projects given to me by the Angels. They are little things each of us can do each month to help the Light and to help others and ourselves, for in helping another we help ourselves. When we are sad or down or depressed reaching out to someone else who is the same or worse brings Light to the world, and to the heart of the receiver as well as the giver and lightens the pain and darkness inside. So if you are experiencing darkness, a feeling of "just get it over with" then here is some thing you can do to help stop that feeling and combat the Darkness that surrounds us.

January:

Tasty Love abounds

Give a cup of warmth and cider or hot coco to someone, you can just buy it and give it away or you can make a small kit with a coffee mug and a mix in it with ribbons on it. Say something like;

"To keep the cold away and lift your spirits, as you do so many others"

February:

"I Appreciate you" eye pads

This month the task is to tell someone how important they are, how much they have touched your life, so they won't be wondering if they made a difference at all. You could just make or buy a pretty card that express's what you have to say or…For the more crafty you could make a few of these and leave them secretly on desks or other places the target person goes to.

Materials Needed:
Soft Material
Batting
Lavender

These are pillows to place over your eyes for resting. Cut out a B shape of soft material and sew together so they fit across the eyes. Fill with cotton batting and Lavender to help with migraines and tired eyes. Leave on desk or mailboxes with a note that says

"I want you to know your works do not go unnoticed. You work hard and I appreciate that. This is to help you rest your tired eyes and help you repair and revive, in this cold month. Thank you for being a big part of it all"

March:

Life renewal

A packet of seeds to be planted, this gives flowers to look forward to. Place them in anything you like, a fancy envelop or a small pot with whatever you like. You can buy seeds or use ones you have collected. With a note that says;

"Life is never the same with your sweet spirit here. Thank you for all the hope you bring"

April:

Angelic Stress reducer

Materials Needed:
A can (small) with lid (optional slit for bank)
Coins for bank or sand and stones or coins to be left in can all the time
Pictures of your favorite angels to be decoupage (light layer of clear drying glue to stick the selected photo, on the can)
Paint
Anything that reminds you of Angels like charms, feathers and so on can be glued to the can as well

Make a small can, decorated with pretty colors and designs (Angels) that can be shaken when someone is feeling very stressed. Since it is tax time you could even make it a small bank and put some change in it with angels on the can to help protect you from the heavy burden of tax day. Shaking it would also relive stress and call the Angels to your side, helping to create a united front. Place a note with the can that says something like:

"Let your stress pour out of your life, like the sound of this can when shaken. Feel it fall away and feel the Angels race to your side. You are loved!"

May:

Flowers Bloom

Give away flowers. They can be handmade tissue flowers or silk ones from the dollar store or real ones. Place in a vase or wrap and put on the persons desk (even a guys.) Flowers help to make people smile and feel loved. Leave a note that says something like:

"You make my world bloom with happiness when you smile"

Materials Needed:

- 1 pack of tissue paper (with 8 sheets)
- Scissors
- Floral wire + scissors

First fold the stack of tissue paper in half and then cut an 8×8 square. So there were 16 layers of 8×8 squares. Next step is to fold the tissue paper in accordion style (about 1 inch for each fold). Place an already cut piece (small) of floral wire and wrapped it around the center to anchor the flower. Next you can leave straight or cut a round tip on each end of the tissue paper.

Last step is to pull each layer of tissue paper up and out gently, one side after the other fluffing as you go, to create the flower.

You can use one color of tissue paper or you can add many color layers as you like, they all become pretty and fun, Add note as discussed above and share the Flowers beauty. Treasures like candy or such can be added to the middle inside of the flower, just wire it in. Your imagination is unlimited here, have fun.

June:

Ringing Protection Bells

Materials Needed:

Jingle bells (small) that ring or a can that you turn into a bell that will ring. Ribbons to hang bell.

Pin is optional

Put all the items together to create a bunch of bells on a string (ribbon). You may leave them silver or paint them. If using cans, paint them and place words of encouragement on them like;

Love
Happiness
Prosperity
Protection

If you want you can paint the bells purple (Higher self) white (purity) pink (unconditional love) add glitter if you like with clear glue. When this is all finished and dry you add a note to the top or bottom of the bell string that says;

"Ring these bells at least once a day, to clear the room and keep negativity away"

July:

Shining Star Reminder

July is a time of Shining so this month the challenge is to give away Stars. They can be any kind of star, they can be made of metal or those wood ones you paint or soaps, even paper or ceramic. Heck place a little glitter on them to make them shine if you like. What ever you feel lead to do, but give away stars. Leave them where the person it is meant for will find them, on a desk, mail them, hang them on a door, anyway you can do this anonymously with a note

Make them small enough to carry in a pocket if you can, and with the note;

Shining Star reminder

Instructions for making clay using flour, salt, and water.

Materials Needed:
2 Cups Flour
1 Cup Salt
2 Tbsp Vegetable Oil
3/4 - 1 Cup Water

Cake food coloring if you like (Purple stars are amazing)
Glitter if you like with glue (diluted like Elmers)
Ribbon to hang

Instructions:

Mix together flour and salt. Add the oil and then slowly add the water and stir until you get a nice clay consistency, add the cake food coloring you like best and mix well.

Once completely mixed, make into Stars being sure to leave a hole at the top for hanging. Bake in a 250 degree oven for approximately 1 hour. This will vary depending on how thick your Stars are. One hint, do not make them too thick or they will crack with baking.

Once cooled you can paint if you didn't add cake food coloring to dough, and add glitter. Cover with a light film of diluted white glue; like Elmers and let dry. Next add the Ribbon and include the following handout with each star

Handout: How to use your Star

This little star was created just for you to carry and hold, and when you think you don't count anymore or have a hard day that leaves you feeling unwanted or unloved take it out and just hold it. Know that someone somewhere (me) thought enough of you to tell you, you are loved, you count and your being here makes the world a better place. You SHINE now and forever.

Now hold this star for as long as you need to chase away the dark thoughts plaguing you and then put away till you need it again. Use as often as needed, the loving energies and strength it contains are ever renewing.

That's all there is to it so you should easily make 3-4 of these this month and give them out to anyone you see that has a need. Thank you for being a part of making the world a better place and thank you for any random acts of kindness you may do, they all count and they all help make a huge difference in the lives of the many they touch. I cant give you a star here but I want to tell you **"You are a wonderful star in this Universe and you Shine"**

August:
Feed the Body the soul will follow

This month is August and this month focuses on the harvest and all that is going on there. The Angels said that this month we are to share food. That could be giving food to those in need or sharing a lunch with a co worker, or the guy on the street that never seems to have enough and is always there. If you are able talk to a local church and make a food box for a family who has a need, drop it off with a note that says;

"You Count, and we care about you and yours"

Did you know there are service families going hungry because they just don't have the money needed. Their other income is away at the war and food is short…is this how we treat our vets and their families? Really is this how we allow **any one** to be treated? Hungry, when all we have to do is reach out and give a bit.

If you are "money tight" and cant give food, then give time to a local food bank or soup kitchen that helps those in need. Giving time of yourself is just as caring and loving (if not more so) as giving a perishable food item.

Just open your eyes and look around, you can see those in need. HELP! An extra sandwich or lunch with their name on it in the fridge at work is nice, (they don't need to know who is helping.) Same for the lady on the bench at the park that seems homeless and alone, sharing a bit of food with her may lift her spirits with the note above that says.

"The world is a better place with you in it"

Maybe you can afford to hand out those food coupons from fast food places, feel free to share them if you like…this month is all about the sharing of the harvest of food.

An apple here or there shared, a drink given to someone in need, a sandwich for a child or even a guy out of work. Kindness is all we are asking and compassion.

September;
Companion time

A time to help those with animals and food for them Take a pet for a walk for a senior, or drop off some food or litter at the doorstep anything like that. Help out with someone's pet, especially those disabled or senior who would be lost without their companion. If all else fails volunteer at a shelter for animals.

OCTOBER:
Make a "See U "Bug Hug

This month of Oct your challenge is simple and easy just walk up to at least 1 person who you sense has been abused, someone who is hurting and down, who is crying inside and wanting to let go and smile at them then tell them that they are truly an Amazing soul and you admire them. Tell them you see how hard they try and what a difference they make and that is to be admired. That's all!

If you are feeling Crafty you could do the following:

Make a "See U "Bug Hug

Create a see you hug with pipe cleaner and googly eyes, with a heart for a tail and a smile from felt. Take your pipe cleaner it can be a straight one or a bump one. If using a bump cleaner you will want 3 or 4 bumps to twist. Place the Googlie eyes on the pipe cleaner with glue and then cut a small smile and heart tail from felt. Glue the smile down under the eyes as well as the heart at the end of the tail. Let dry. Once dry twist this around a pencil or pen or coffee cup or such. Next write a note that says something like

"I See you, You count! From your See your own hug bug"

Step 1 = Pick out what Pipe Cleaner You will be using

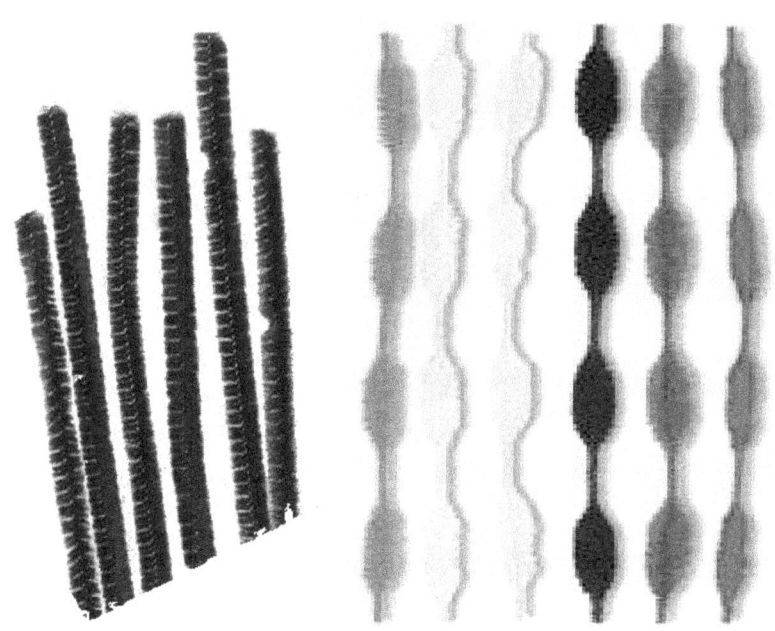

Step 2= Get the Googlie eyes and glue ready. Cut the felt into a small smile and heart tail

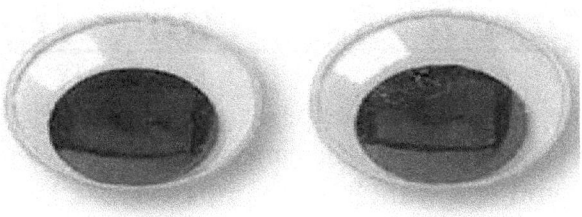

Step 3 = Glue it all together and let dry. Leave enough on body-tail to twist around something

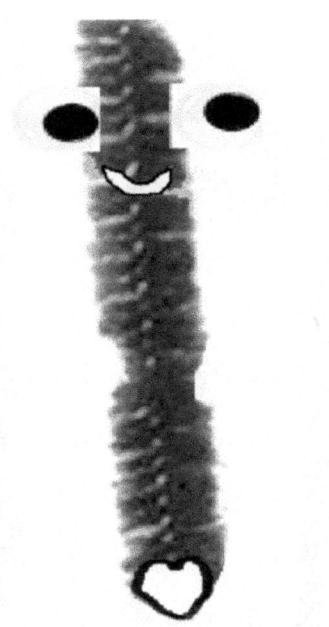

    Watch how they change! Watch their spirit rise and how the smile touches their heart, watch what your words do to lift the pain and chase back the darkness. Then Dear Ones, feel how it makes you feel, how it helps you rise from the pit of apathy and sadness to caring and hope and share that kindness again and again as you can if you like. So there is your Oct Challenge reach out and do an ***ACT OF LIGHT***

November:
You Rock reminder

OK this month's (NOV) *Act of Light* is fun and easy. Go find at least one stone, it can be pebble sized which can be carried or paper weight sized which can be used to on a desk.

Materials Needed:
- A smooth Stone
- Paint

1. Clean the stone good from dirt.

2. Then paint, glue or draw eyes and a smiling mouth on the stone, if you are artistic fix it up even more.

3. Next make a small tag that reads **"YOU ROCK!"**

4. Now give the stone and tag to someone who is in need of a smile or something to lift their spirits. You can leave it anonymously or give it to them one on one.

Do this at least once this month, more is fun and believe me as corny as it sound people like them. It's a nice reminder that someone notices you and thinks a lot of you. In your pocket where you can clutch it for shots of much needed self esteem to sitting out on your desk to remind you what a winner you are. The more you make and give the more you will want to make .

December:
Warm fuzzies

Dec. Challenge is to help others in times of need, to warm them so they feel a part of something, to make them feel needed and wanted. This is a cold month usually, it nips at the finger and toes. It chips away at the heart making the lonely more alone and the neglected feeling even more unwanted.

This is the time of year bright packages go by that make many remember that they will not be at gatherings on any special day, nor will there be any special gift to say **I love you** for them. Your job is to lift that feeling and replace it with a feeling of warm cozy love, its easy.

Give someone you don't even know the gift of gloves to warm the fingers or a scarf to wrap around them. They will remember someone cared each time they put it on. If you can, you can even do a blanket to help someone know they are wrapped in protective love from your heart, anything like that which warms and keeps them remembering they are not now or ever truly alone.

Now I know money is tight but you could easily get nice items at second hand stores and give them away or **make** scarves or anything like that, let your mind create ideas for you. There are no hard and fast rules here just give it all in love and lift the spirit

Be sure to put a card that says something like;

"As this gift warms your body, know that my love is there to warm your soul and touch your heart. You are so wonderful and deserve a warm fuzzy"

Give to those in need the material poor and the spiritual poor for all may be hurting at the hole inside them, at this time of year. Lets us all unite and Light the way for everyone to feel loved, cared about and cozy warm this month!

Personal Notes & Experiences

Personal Notes & Experiences

Concluding Section

*This is a reprint from **Stop Kickin' My Chair**, yet I felt it belonged here in this book as well....*

This page is special, it is for those that are looking to connect with ALBs, to invite them into their life and to fight back the Darkness. Its not hard to do, pretty simple really. Give it a try and watch for signs of their being there. A feeling, a sensation, a smell, maybe even a voice or a person who comes from no where. Angels are all about us, waiting to be asked in, just ask for their positive love and direction and be ready for miracles!!!

How to Ask the Angels for Their Guidance in Your Life

© Lady Wolfen Mists 1-11-2005

Angels please guide my words and works this day that I walk in the Lighted path of the Goddess and God.

Lift me up and keep me and all I hold dear safe and protected with your wings about me and in the hands of the Lady.

Keep all negativity from my presence and allow me to help others and make their life a bit brighter and better.

Let me be kind, compassionate and give me wisdom and strength.

I declare my soul to the Lighted Path and my essence to the Lady and Lord of Light.

Let it be so for all the days of my existence and I ask that you as guides and protectors walk at my side.

Personal Notes & Experiences

Personal Notes & Experiences

Personal Notes & Experiences

Here Now
Silver Hoofs & Paws Projects

CHILDREN'S CORNER BOOKS
The Adventures of Knobbly Vol 1 By Addy Venture & A Bud Dee
The adventures of Knobbly the squirrel, his Faery and Forest friends. Knobbly's life as he ventures from home in the Misty Mountains.

The Adventures of Knobbly Vol 2 By Addy Venture & A Bud Dee
More Stories about Knobbly

INSPIRATIONAL BOOKS
Stop Kicking My Chair By Lady Wolfen Mists
Working With Angels and the messages given to her over the years, some never before shared

Tools Of Light By Lady Wolfen Mists
Tools given to her for the world to use from the Angels

Wiccan Religion BOOKS
WOLFEN WICCA: A beginners Journey to Pre-dedication By Lady Wolfen Mists
Wolfen Wicca: This is a beginners guide to Wolfen Wicca, step by step easy to follow

Wolfen Wicca 2: Our Walk Onward To Initiation By Lady Wolfen Mists
Continue your Journey to1st degree level, lots of aspects covered from the wolf beside you to past life andmany otherareas

More in the works……

http://www.silverhoofs.com

Purchase Books from
http://www.lulu.com/spotlight/silverhoofs

Our Website
You can always contact Lady Wolfen there and she will answer as she has time

http://www.silverhoofs.com